This is the true story of Suzanne Boylston Cusack growing up in a middle-class family in Far Rockaway, Long Island, NY, in the 1950s. She was brought up with a strong faith and the discipline of Catholic high school. In her family life, she grew up surrounded by the hurts, fears, and disillusionments of living with her dad's weekend alcoholism. She vowed never to drink, but at age 18, she found her way to the glamor of working for a prominent firm in Rockefeller Center, and the advertising world, long drinking lunches, and after-hour working parties. She became very successful materially, but at the age of 28, lost herself. Her mom, quietly seeing her daughter follow in Dad's footsteps, prayed very hard. Since her mom is Catholic and believes in the magical powers of blessed holy water, she began pouring some in Sue's drinks whenever she could. Suddenly, the miracle occurred and Sue called the Alcoholics Anonymous, 24-hour helpline on June 3, 1969.

And so, from that *Holy Water in My Scotch* carries us through to the present as she deals with widowhood and carrying on her soul mate's mission…solely responsible for maintaining the 100 acres, 85-bed treatment center they began together with the treasured staff of 50, who are still family to her. Her faith and determination will inspire all ages for all times. She considers herself blessed to be able to do what she loves with the ones she loves and works hands-on helping the addicted, and their families find help and hope daily.

She just celebrated 50 years sober on June 4, 2019.

Dedicated to:

Mom, who never gave up on me, whose intense faith in the power of prayer and holy water led me to hope and help.

My little brother, Jimmy, who, along with his wife, Maureen, helped me through that first tough year of sobriety.

My best friend, soul mate, husband…my everything, Jim, the inspiration behind this book.

My sister, Joan, my forever friend.

My traveling team, my flexible flier siblings and in-laws: Joan, Steve, Jack, Elaine, Tom, and Ann—family who were dear friends as well as family.

All my treasured nieces and nephews, part of our sweetest memories.

My Villa family, present and past, many who have passed on but each one leaving their mark on my heart and being part of who I am today.

My first AA sponsor, Margaret G. drove me to detox. in 1969 and just presented me with my 50 year sober coin last year!. She is 95 years young and still goes to meetings!

My years of 12-step families from Long Island to Kerhonkson, who have been, and still are, my strength and support.

My step-children, who treasure and love our Jim with me and have truly become my family.

Our prayer group of friends who met faithfully every week as we supported each other through life's crises. Thank you, Carmen, Casey, Cathy, and Dick.

My cousins from California, Texas, Virginia, and Long Island, who show me how to age gracefully...and share ancient family memories and secrets that no one else knows.

Suzanne Boylston Cusack

HOLY WATER IN MY SCOTCH

From Despair to Hope

AUSTIN MACAULEY PUBLISHERS™

LONDON · CAMBRIDGE · NEW YORK · SHARJAH

Ordering Information:
Quantity sales: special discounts are available on quantity purchases by corporations, associations, and others. For details, contact the publisher at the address below.

Publisher's Cataloguing-in-Publication data
Cusack, Suzanne Boylston
Holy Water in My Scotch

ISBN 9781647500979 (Paperback)
ISBN 9781647500962 (Hardback)
ISBN 9781647500986 (ePub e-book)

Library of Congress Control Number: 2020904921

www.austinmacauley.com/us

First Published (2020)
Austin Macauley Publishers LLC
40 Wall Street, 28th Floor
New York, NY 10005
USA

mail-usa@austinmacauley.com
+1 (646) 5125767

Acknowledgement

To the Dominican sisters of Amityville, who hired Jim and gave him a chance to restart his dream of a haven for alcoholics and open a new chapter of my life.

The Murray family, especially Barbara, who helped Jim edit his book and kept urging me to write my story…thank you, Barbara, for being my best fan and cheerleader.

John Murray, who kept encouraging me to write and whose friendship with Mary Higgins Clark led me to Austin Macauley.

The Peters family: first Ken, who helped Jim with his eyesight, and recently, Claudia Ragni, for opening doors for the Villa mission to move forward.

Sister Peggy and Sister Mary-Ann, for giving me a Christmas gift of a New Beginning's retreat I didn't know I needed.

Thank you to my new friends at New Beginnings, who have grieved with me and shown me truly new beginnings…thank you for pushing me to write again, find what was buried, and turn it into this book, which we hope will help many.

Thank you to all my Union brothers and sisters, who loved Jim over the years and have helped me keep the Villa going after he passed away. You visited us, kept us involved and encouraged me to make the trip to your huge Vegas conference. You honored Jim and the Villa there and our history with you with so much love and accolades and made me feel so supported and welcomed. You too are a big part of this book, encouraging me to keep going. Thank you.

Also, to Diana and team at The Cottage in Ellenville, NY, for performing their magic on hairstyle and nails to keep me going.

To photographer Michael Gold, for patience and expertise in making one look good but real.

To our loyal and supportive accounting firm/family, from Vincent Panettieri Sr. who donated their services when we began 47 years ago and on now to Vincent Jr. who continues their love and care, thank you team SCHULTHEIS and PANETTIERI

I was a surprise package to my parents, as my folks tell me. They were third cousins who met at a social event, continued to party together, and finally married.

To narrate my life story, I must give you a background on the family in which I was born. Not a "normal family" (if there is such a thing), this family was a big part of who I am today.

Mom was married to a prominent attorney. She had a fairytale book wedding with the love of her life. Shortly after they were married, the Almighty blessed them with a beautiful little girl who later won a contest for looking like Shirley Temple. Three years later, Mom's beloved husband died suddenly, and the incident shattered her life. There was a big mystery about his death as it occurred on the Labor Day weekend. He was away, supposedly on business, had a sudden stroke or embolism, and died instantly. To this day, neither Mom, nor my sister, nor anyone ever found out, nor did anyone question. Mom went into shock, and her sister, our aunt, helped a lot. It shattered my sister's perfect life as well, and she learned to cope as best she could. Mom was there in body, but it was a terrible time for them all. Drinking was always a coping mechanism in all the family histories involved, so we know it was to play a part in the decision-making and fate of all concerned.

Here's where I prepared to enter the picture…

Mom met my dad at one of the many beach parties in the Rockaways; they enjoyed drinking and partying and brought Mom's daughter along most of the time. Joanne was about five when Mom and my dad married. My dad was forty-two at the time, in the Navy, a drinker, and never held a decent job. He grew to love my sister as his own daughter. For the next five years of her life, she was the center of their world, and Dad settled into a newspaper advertising position.

After that, he drank on weekends only as a means to control it and, from what I gather, managed a reasonably good life.

Five years passed and suddenly… SURPRISE! They were going to have a baby!!!

I think they had a ton of mixed emotions there… Dad was then forty-seven, with periods of binge drinking thrown in from time to time. Mom was forty-one and, in those days, pretty old to have a baby. Add to the mix, one I never knew they worried about; they were third cousins (once removed). It caused them both (without ever talking about it as no one communicated too well in those days) to fear genetic deformities. Fortunately, except for the addiction gene, both my younger brother (another surprise to them, four years after me!) and I escaped any apparent mental or physical deformities.

And so, on Thursday, March 6, 1941, little Suzanne (Suzy) Boylston entered the world at St. Joseph's Hospital in Far Rockaway, N. Y. My mother was thrilled, as, in those days, new mothers and babies were kept a week in the hospital, cared for, and catered to, and my mom felt it was a great vacation as well!

Mom and Dad had not done much vacationing. His drinking had insidiously affected their life and marriage. Though no one talked about it, it just became a way of living that one learned to endure. When I was born, there would have been a dramatic change in my sister's life, as Mom began to put all her love and attention into my wellbeing. I cried incessantly; they tell me, perhaps affected by all the fear and negativity I was born into, or just plain colicky. I soon grew up to be very emotionally attached to Mom as Dad didn't know what to do with a baby. My sister would have resented all the attention she had and then lost when her dad died.

So here I am, trying to make sense of it all as I grow up. Looking back, I learn how to stuff the fears and tensions. Many memories are vague and not clear if they are mine or simply told to me.

As I grew up, they made me feel pretty special; until one day, they scooped me up to stay in Queens Village with my cousins. They treated me great, but I missed Mom and when I got home, my world upended with the arrival of my baby brother! He was so cute but took Mom over. And I began to develop a nervous stomach (it was where all my tensions landed) and the life-long battle with IBS (Irritable Bowel Syndrome).

Looking back, our lives appeared relatively normal…a stay-at-home mom, Dad out to work every day and home for dinner, my sister aged fifteen, brother aged one, and myself aged five. Money was very tight and created a lot of tension. Mom wanted to give us everything she could, often running up debts, charging beyond her means. Many arguments went through the emotions of the family when my older sister began acting out, storming out of the house. Mom was in tears, and I was hurt for Mom…only later realized how rejected, lost, and alone my sister would have felt. Dad never said much, felt his responsibility was to put food on the table. Without any friendship between the two, we were beginning to see not much of marriage there. Mom was still so in love with her first husband, who became a mirage to her. How was it that I knew so much about him? When he died on a Labor Day weekend, Mom relived that loss every year.

My dad clearly could never live up to him. He drank to escape the empty life they had. Sometimes, Mom joined him, and I remember being disgusted with both of them. As I got older, I vowed never to drink or date anyone who did. I often got angry with my mom for staying with Dad though she had no choice, being a homemaker with no money. It was here that I became disillusioned with a lot of things. Marriage was a trap and not for me. I didn't say that to myself but set myself up to pursue a career (in advertising like Dad) as Dad's role of going out, working, and coming home looked much better than Mom's. Though we all benefited having the joys of a stay-at-home-mom, she was the best and always there for us, cooking and cleaning, but she never had a life. As we got older, we resented her still wanting to control our lives and felt sorry for her and angry because we had become her only life.

Along the way, then, at age nine, my sister was nineteen, met someone, and married. A year later, I was an aunt at age ten and began seeing what looks great at first, but soon saw another life of dedication to discipline, not one of choice.

Later, my brother and I grew up in a home that was OK during the week but full of anger and drinking on weekends. Holidays were always very unpredictable… Mom would do so much to make Christmas special, decorating the tree, buying us as much as she could, and my poor dad was just a fixture in holidays, drinking through them. I loved him and knew I was precious to him and daddy's little girl, but he just couldn't show it. We later learned that he had grown up in a fatherless home. His dad died early of alcohol-related pneumonia and was raised by a mom, who wasn't very loving, and a tyrant of a grandfather. It then made sense to me. He only lived what he learned. He never knew how to love and be loved and alcohol-soothed, he made it all go away when it hurt too much.

The most stable part of my life was my four years of all-girls Catholic High School, an academy on Thirty-fourth St. in Manhattan. I assumed the role of the Family Hero, doing well in school and making my parents proud. Mom was my best self-esteem booster…steady and constant…no matter what I did, she thought it was great. Had to learn later, that wasn't always the case with everyone else!

Why choose a school to travel to by a one-hour train ride every day for four years? One may ask! My three best girlfriends from grammar school in Far Rockaway were all going there, and we wanted to stick together. Religious sisters had taught us, and they were tough. Uniforms had to be perfect, on time every day from 8:30 a.m. to 3:00 p.m., and four hours' homework every night. Discipline and hard work created a haven of safety and caring and the only stable thing in my life at the time. Those nuns gave me the work ethic, and it has been a trademark of my life and career and toughened me up to face any and all challenges in life. I am forever grateful to those four years and all those tough nuns! Home was never predictable and was all a part of the family tension most weekends and holidays. Drinking had a hold on all, in various stages and times, stealing true love and family life from the picture.

The sad part was that we didn't know, understand, or see it. We accepted it as the norm and learned to endure.

As I began my last year of high school, my dad, who was then about sixty-four, became very ill and was told he needed a colostomy due to cancer of the colon. The procedure involved complete removal of the colon, leaving a colostomy bag outside the body. It was devastating for us all as a family, as I look back now, in so many ways. There was no second opinion sought. No one knew enough to do that. It destroyed my dad's manhood, and they told Mom she was so young, and they felt bad for her. My dad would need his own room as enduring the odor and tending to it would be tough. Mom was to move in and share my room. It just "happened" and at sixteen, I was sharing a bed and room with Mom trying to do homework and keep up the grades. My sister and husband helped wherever they could. I was too young to fully understand, except this added to our family tension and fears. Dad's brothers visited, and the seriousness hit us all. On top of it, we were poor with little income to take care of nurses needed, etc. My uncles helped and got us through the surgery and hospitalization.

After Dad came home with this nightmare of a life sentence, with absolutely no counseling help in those days, we were still without much income, and he had to go back to work as best he could. He lived quite a few years with the colostomy bag, and the odors were sometimes unbearable. He still drank beer on weekends as he was depressed, and once started, he couldn't stop. The drinking created more havoc with his condition. I remember isolating in our room or staying at friends as much as I could. It's sometimes vague to me how we got through it all! Holidays and birthdays came and went, and Dad was sometimes OK and sometimes not. School was my safety outlet and kept me busy all week. I started dating the boy across the street, and he became a good friend as well.

With Dad and our income adversely affected, they told me and realized I must work part-time after school in the city to earn my own tuition to finish high school. Tuition was $18 per month. I did it, but disillusionment and hopelessness set in. I had applied and been accepted to a few colleges and had been looking forward to going, but there was no money. We didn't look for loans in those days. Either you had parents, wealthy enough to help, or you worked your way through. I had an offer by an aunt who wanted to pay my way through four years of college, but she was known to be a dominating person and made it sound very grueling. By then, I had begun working after school in an exciting printing firm, where my work ethic attracted praise and love by all. I had the taste of earning my own way. I loved the independence but was also shocked that after four years of Catholic school, married men (twice my age) would ask me out. I never went, but what an eye-opener!

Once I turned eighteen and had my first drink (though I said I never would), I loved the relaxation and magic it gave me. I never had any stomach problems with one or two after work. IBS became a thing of the past. It also opened a part of me that changed my thinking...a new me. I went from the safe boy across the street to a frivolous vacation with girlfriends in a resort in Pa. I fell for the handsome lifeguard, who I thought was attending Lehigh Univ. for engineering. What a shock to find he was studying to become an Episcopalian Minister, but, by then, I was addicted to him. Brought him home to my Irish Catholic family, who then thought I was doomed to hell. Dad was upset and worried about me. I never felt so torn, and after an eight-month affair including an engagement on New Year's Eve, we broke up, not over religion but over his inability to be faithful. So, I had my heart broken, had a few more drinks to smooth the hurt, and went on with my life.

So, after graduation, I entered the business world...and stayed with the printing firm until age twenty-one. I outgrew the printing firm, and the owner there encouraged me to take a six-week Speed Writing course (a precursor to TEXTING TODAY). I went twice a week, at night, after work on Forty-second St. in New York City and took the subway home to Far Rockaway, where I lived with Mom and Dad. I passed the course with flying colors and a certificate that armed me with the expertise of Shorthand! I set out to find the next big job.

In May 1962, I went for an interview at a life-changing job at a well-known firm on Fifth Avenue, opposite St. Patrick's Cathedral. Dressed for success, with prep from a friend, who attended an elite secretarial school, I wore a blue wool suit, white gloves, and a small hat!!! I was interviewed for Secretary to Sales Promotion Manager at $150 per week with Blue Cross Health Insurance – all a gift in those days for a young career woman. My whole family was so proud, and Dad enjoyed every minute, too, of his little girl's success. I went across the street after the interview, to St. Patrick's, to pray I get the job. Yes! I was the lucky one selected!!! I found an attraction to the instant gratification of earning good money and being able to help my parents, who were always struggling, as I still lived at home. They needed me, I said, but I also needed them, and as they were getting older, I felt I had to care for them and give them a better life. I loved the excitement and the taste of New York City, the advertising world, and creating my own future.

October 1962

I began friendship with my boss (twenty years my senior and separated from his wife). He became an attraction, and addiction and for seven years enabled me to see the NYC life and the world in an exciting way. He taught me so much about life and the world…a fantasy friendship that only saw each other at our best. He was not real love or husband material but part of my growing to who I was to become. We both lived in two separate worlds that enabled me to live a double life, of which I was also very guilty and ashamed…being the good daughter at home, on weekends and holidays, taking care of Mom and Dad and never able to share that part of my life. There, I saw the pattern of selecting men and relationships that protected me from commitment…saying I want the husband and family with many kids but not really. Growing up around many unhappy marriages, I enjoyed being on the outside, or at least I thought so until I found REAL LOVE much later in my life. I wouldn't have known it if I didn't live through all this.

My boss also encouraged me to grow and continue to learn. He loved me as much as he was capable of, and was my biggest cheerleader in pushing me to model once for display ad and take up copywriting.

My business world, as did my school world, kept me grounded as I coped with all the sadness and grief in my family. It kept me balanced and centered. I can see now that it helped me handle things. The big thing working against me was my own slowly and insidiously developing alcoholism. Most of my work meetings revolved around a drink at lunch, a drink after work, a growing dependency to meet the Boss and relax or meet friends in the same position as us, and relax over a drink.

Then, suddenly, I was faced with my dad's next and fatal illness. All these years, Mom and I were still sharing a room at home, and Dad was living with an awful colostomy and often too sick to drink. By the way, his doctor, who insisted Dad have his entire colon removed, came to us later and said it was a mistake. He did not have cancer! It was another heartbreaker we all faced and could do nothing. The doctor said he was sorry. No one sued in those days, and we sure learned to "accept the things we cannot change." Looking back now, I get such courage from seeing how and with what all my parents dealt. In spite of everything, they prayed, said their rosaries, and believed in a God…they gave me that, and I guess there is a lot to the song Faith of our Fathers…inner strength…and guts… They taught me a lot in their suffering.

Later, Dad had cancer of the jaw. He had been to the dentist with a sore in his mouth, a short while ago, and then this. Did he smoke? Oh yes! And he did as long as he could.

He was still working to put food on the table. Most of my friends worked, lived at home, and turned in a rent the folks saved for them. But, not in my family. My parents needed my $50 per week to pay the bills. Dad sold newspaper advertising on Long Island. He needed to work. Mom even went out and worked for our local cleaner to pitch in. And then, this.

I was twenty-five years old, and Dad was sixty-six, terminally ill with cancer of the jaw.

From what we all know today about alcoholism; we can state Dad was an alcoholic. We loved him but despised his drinking. As the cancer developed and progressed, he could no longer drink, and this new illness brought us closer as a family. We (my brother, my sister, and I) took turns juggling jobs as family, as we helped Dad face the dreaded radiation therapy twice weekly for over a year. As the cancer took its toll, Dad became "old" quickly. He had to sell out his share of the newspaper business he owned. Then his worst fears became a reality. He was old, terminally ill, and had very little funding to fall back on.

In spite of the cancer, he still worked for the newspaper he once partly owned. He felt he had to. He needed the money, and through it all, he never complained. I remember him going out every day to sell newspaper ads when all he could eat was malted milkshakes. He could no longer chew as the cancer progressed. But he still felt useful.

Then one day, he came home and told us he was fired. They hired a younger man to begin work right away. Dad was no longer "needed." No retirement dinner, no gift. No dignity preserved. It crushed his spirit forever and our hearts with it. Dad was then old and sick, no longer useful, and heartbroken. Dad died eight months later; surrounded by love, he had finally enjoyed, loved, and respected by his family for his courage and strength…stigmatized by the society for growing old and ill. The episode taught me to be kind to employees who age in their place. We move them around until they decide to retire or whatever. It helped me with all our relatives and friends and prepared me to handle it as smoothly as Dad and Mom did.

Now, we get to my decline, to the final stage of my alcoholism.

While my brother, my sister, and I had seen and been hurt by our dad's drinking, we had no clue about alcoholism – the disease – and so, each of us in our own way slipped on the slippery road there. We all sought solace in drinking away our grief over Dad's death.

My sister thought I should take a trip to Florida to get away from it all.

I did and simply drank away the whole time there. Then, to our family doctor, Dr. Schwartz, unaware also of the dangers of alcohol, with or without medication, prescribed me Valium (mother's little helpers): 5 mg as needed.

Before long, I was addicted, drinking in the evening, and taking Valium in the morning for the anxiety. However, nothing helped calm the fears or helped the depression.

In 1968, Mom was diagnosed with congestive heart failure. I resigned from my job to take the summer off and care for Mom. Doctor suggested Mom had a scotch with dinner every night, and of course, I joined her and continued after I took her to bed.

My money was running out, and thus, I applied for my next DREAM JOB – the one I hoped to get with encouragement from my old boss and paramour, whom I was still seeing. I was interviewed for Assistant to Advertising Director of a Corporate Service to Lawyers firm on Park Avenue, Forty-eighth St., NYC.

I was hired!!! But soon after, I found myself in over my head. My new boss drank daily and had me covering for him; our Joint Secretary is a Valium addict, and since I was able to get a bottle of sixty any time I wanted at my pharmacy for $5. A bottle, and we became fast friends.

Pretty soon, my boss paramour got tired of my drinking and calling him at all hours. I began having lunch alone. I disliked myself as I then NEEDED to drink and felt guilty as to how much I needed to refuel with a large martini – the preference. I still commuted between the city and Far Rockaway, but often woke up on the train at 6:00 a.m., seeing the time, but not sure if I was going home or coming in to work. I was getting very scared then too.

In January 1969, I saw a life-changing poster on the subway…

"If you think you have a drinking problem, call AA Intergroup."

One day, I wrote the number down and took it home.

The Moment of Truth

It was a warm June morning, June 2, 1969. My girlfriend, Bess, and I were on the Long Island Railroad, heading back to our jobs in NYC after a long Memorial Day weekend, partying in the Hamptons. We were both emotional-pain-carrying members of the empty life club, living two lives for many years. The Valium I took that morning didn't calm the panic and fear, nor did the bottle of Dewar's scotch I carried in my big bag. The shakes, panic, and fear took over, and I told Bess I was getting off in Jamaica and heading home for the day. I couldn't find a cab and took a chance to hitch a ride. I had never done this before but was desperate. That man turned out to be a God-sent Angel in disguise, as he drove me right to my door in Far Rockaway…miraculously safe and sound. When you hear of the nightmares we see today…someone up there was looking out for me. I felt bad physically, but the emotional self-hate was worse. As I arrived home to Mom, it was her birthday, and I had no gift, but one rose I had managed to pick up on the train station. Her look was one of both disgust and relief, as at least I was safe. I loved my mom dearly and was always thoughtful about her and close to her.

Realizing how far away addiction had taken me from my core values and love of family, it finally hit me hard that day. My mother's face… I was causing her the same pain my dad had…knowing how she worried…it finally got through. Later, I found out she had been quietly pouring HOLY WATER IN MY SCOTCH for months. And she glowed that God heard her prayers, finally, and that my asking for help on her birthday was the best gift she could get.

I called AA Intergroup for help that afternoon. They offered me a few ways to help: an AA meeting, a hospital or treatment center. In 1969, there was not a whole lot available, and the stigma for women was significant. Knowing I could no longer stop drinking on my own, I found out I had five days' coverage in a hospital on Long Island. There, they would help me detoxify and learn about my disease. My brother took the phone and set up for them to send two AA volunteers – a man and a woman – who would be available the next day at 5:00 p.m. They told him if I had trouble not drinking the following morning, he could give me a drink – good thing as I woke up with shakes, sweats, and fears: the worst ever. My brother found a pint of gin in our basement. I finished it and got all dressed up to begin my new journey that was – with the grace of God and my mother's prayers – to last for fifty years to this day.

Five days in the hospital, of course, were not enough. Today, we know that Valium withdrawal is an agonizing, emotional, panicky withdrawal that can take up to six months. In those days, my doctor and many others said it was not addictive! My roommate was a 70-year-old woman who had many, many visits to the hospital. Her family was disgusted, and she no longer had much hope.

But she was there and was a lasting impression for me… Something hit me… "Sure you can drink again, Sue, but this will be your life…if you live that long…" It was an eye-opener!

I also met a woman twenty years my senior, the wife of a dentist with six children.

She, too, was addicted to alcohol and Valium and was going next to a rehab center in Glen Spey, NY. We became friends, and I also was offered a choice of aftercare rehab. One was at the cost of $100 per week in Connecticut…the other where my friend was going…only $65 per week…so I chose that. It was the start of a friendship that lasted for over forty-five years. My friend, Sally, had to go home and take care of six kids and an angry husband. I was lucky for being single and having the support of a mom and a great little brother. My sister had been my drinking buddy and was still drinking.

Little did I know that the choice of a rehab was the defining plan for my life and future.

My brother and mom drove me to Glen Acre on June 9, 1969, and I met and shook hands for the first time with Mr. Jim Cusack, who was the Director of the Lodge. He seemed nice enough. However, it was a Sunday afternoon, and we came in on an AA meeting, full of what appeared a lot of old people, talking about an "ulcer room." So, it was a bit scary. Then, I met another older woman who was in charge of the women. She had a squeaky mid-west accent and didn't seem too friendly. Soon after, my friend Sally, mother of the six kids, came up to welcome me, and I felt relieved. She said it was nice there, and she would show me around.

The first week was tough. We were checked out by a local doctor from a little town in Shohola, Pa. And I remember my friend Sally and I felt good that he didn't think we were "the Glen Acre type." I guess he didn't think we looked like alcoholics, in whatever way he perceived them, but the fact remained that we WERE the type as we surely needed to be there. They gave us no medication…just lots of good food and meetings. I cried a lot from emotional withdrawal, could only sleep an hour at a time, and dreaded the nights. Their only answer to no sleep was very unsympathetic, "You never die from lack of sleep!" We had to be up for breakfast at 7:30 a.m. every day, attend a two-hour group meeting every morning, and smoking was allowed any time (hard to believe). Every day, I was asked, "Do you think you are an alcoholic?" Every day, I answered, "I didn't know yet." The word choked in my throat as my whole family drank, and the stigma, especially for women, was dismal. Mom told everyone I had a nervous breakdown, and that was acceptable.

My Park Avenue Lawyer's job allowed a disability for "anxiety neurosis." So, I was able to stay up to six weeks at $65 per week.

We had to listen to Fr. John Doe records (yes, vinyl records) every day at 5:00 p.m. He droned on and on, and I wasn't too impressed. But funny enough, there was one thing he said often, and it stuck in my brain and helped me through many tough times for fifty years. He repeated these words over and over, "ACTION IS THE MAGIC WORD." Yes! It sure is! And it has kept me going whenever I wanted to take the lazy way out. After all the deaths and losses of those close to me…when I wanted just to stay in bed and never get up…those words would resonate in my brain…and I would dress up and show up to be wherever Higher Power needed me to be. "Act as if," "it works if you work It," "gratitude attitude overcomes everything," Fr. John Doe had it all in spite of my liking him or not wanting to hear it.

Then, a few weeks into Glen Acre, we graduated to being taken to an outside meeting by volunteers. So, Sally and I were all excited…being sophisticated Long Islanders and city girls…we were going out!!! Oh my, it was not what we expected! When we got to our first outside meeting in Milford, Pa, with a group of potato growing farmers and dairy cow folks, we heard sobriety in their terms. Every meeting was an eating one with home-baked treats and talk of tension in growing potatoes, to getting up at 3:30 a.m. to milk the cows! It showed us a different world, but AA was working, no matter where we went.

Slowly, we learned about the beautiful foundation and way of life of the Twelve Steps through Jim's brilliant daily program. He had begun this program in 1965 when he was led to the Lodge by some retired policemen.

He felt he had a calling to help other alcoholics find the way of life he had found after ten, tough years. He felt that if people could take time out from their daily lives and give at least two weeks to learning about the disease of alcoholism and addiction, they would have a chance to stay sober. He wanted to teach them that they were GOOD PEOPLE WITH A BAD DISEASE. And then learn to apply the foundation of the fellowship and the Twelve Steps to stay sober. A day at a time, with meetings across the world. He went out to a Treatment Center in Minnesota, the leader in our field at that time and one of the few places around, to learn all he could. He then came back, applied, and added to it as he developed his unique style. He became an early pioneer recognized by the NYC Police Dept. and other companies for his methods of intervention and adding treatment of the families to the mix.

Sally and I were blessed to have chosen this program as it gave us both the foundation we needed to go out into the world and stay sober. Sally went home to her family of husband and six children, and I went home to Mom.

We both had sponsors, as they taught us at the center to have, who we checked in with every day. I had both: a tough sponsor and an easy sponsor.

When I went home, my brother was engaged and planning a wedding. My brother and my future sister-in-law were strong support for me. They went to meetings with me occasionally and were very proud of my sobriety.

They even planned for me to be a bridesmaid at their wedding, but I was nervous about staying sober. Thus, they invited my sponsors as well.

Mom found it hard not to worry and be able to trust me if I was a few minutes late, but I gave her permission to call my sponsors to relieve her and free me of nagging.

My sister missed me drinking with her, and looked down, at first, on my going away to rehab. She was working hard raising a family, struggling with a husband who didn't know what was happening, but who was the first person to call me an alcoholic! He didn't know what an alcoholic was, but he knew my drinking was out of hand and didn't like my negative influence on his wife. They both thought my going away and ultimately resigning from my city job was a cop-out, and my going to the Lodge was like going on vacation! Little did they know. When they came to visit me, they both needed a drink, we just ignored it and stayed on the course. Mom was my buddy and wouldn't let anyone drink at home with me, and that didn't go over too well.

When I first returned home, I had no job, was too nervous to drive, and made my meetings my priority. I joined the Valley Stream Group of AA in Valley Stream,

NY, and they became my surrogate family for guidance and support.

I had to bring the cake every week as they got me involved in service to belong. Another young woman and I were the youngest in the group, and everyone helped us. They were very strict about women with women and very protective of us both. In the mornings, I called looking for work, went on the unemployment line for a few hours and left…no matter what job, I needed to work. Right down the street from unemployment was the Long Island newspaper, where my dad had once worked. I knew the owner. I went in and told her the truth that I had been away for alcoholism treatment and then needed a job. She gave me one for $50 per week, of selling advertising space, part-time to start with, and eventually, a second job in insurance claims. Together, they paid $100 per week! I couldn't wait to get to my Twelve Step group family that night and tell them. I was like a big kid with a new toy. I was the big advertising executive from Fifth Avenue and Park Avenue. Having made $12,000 a year back then, I was ECSTATIC and grateful to get these two jobs. My family group and my own family were thrilled too as it was something I could do and stay sober. Next, my brother at the bank, where he worked, had an older man with a great car offer: one-time owner, 1965 green Chevrolet for sale…at only $750. I was able to get a bank loan and pay it off at $67 per month. Then, I was back in business: twenty-nine-years-old, two part-time jobs, a car, and a fantastic support system…just like they taught us at the Lodge.

Meanwhile, my friend Sally found similar great support in a Group only a half-hour away from me. She had struggles coping with raising six children and having a husband who didn't want her drinking, but it shouldn't interfere with him having his 6:00 p.m. martini every day!!!

Rather than argue, she told her sponsors, and they showed up taking turns every night as he drank his martini, and they all chatted. Either he got tired of seeing them every night, or he gave up martinis, but it all worked out!

As for the addiction I had to my older friend of seven years, I never called him or any of my drinking friends in the city. I knew I had to stay away from them and treat them all like the first drink, and by the grace of God, I did. One girlfriend, who worked at an advertising Agency and looked out for me, kept trying to get me to meet her. I ignored the calls, and years later, she ended up in our treatment center. She forgave me, but I am sorry to say she died from alcoholism, and still had the beautiful sublet apartment on First Avenue, where we all hung out. She couldn't stay sober as hard as we tried. But for the grace of God, sobriety means a lot to me, and it's truly a gift I treasure, above all, every day.

Now back to Jim Cusack at the Lodge: He married the owner of the Lodge, sometime prior to my going there, and inherited great step-kids we all adored. Everyone loved our families as well and Sally, and I often went back there to speak out of gratitude for the foundation we received there. Jim saw how well I was doing, and on one of my visits there, he introduced me to a nice Irishman, Jimmy C., who had just completed a few months sober. Jimmy was a cute Irish bartender from Queens, and we enjoyed each other's company right away. We dated and had fun, but before long, Jimmy was drinking again. I had been taking him to meetings against one sponsor's advice, and then, nine months sober, I found myself lying and not telling her the truth. Fortunately, I was still close to Sally and spoke to her a lot. Luckily for me, though I was heartbroken at the time because I liked the sober Jimmy, the drinking Jimmy left me and went back to his old girlfriend. All in God's plan as they eventually married, had a baby, and he never could stay sober and died a few years later – from alcoholism.

At the time, my group didn't criticize or judge me but was supportive and so helpful. Three months later, on June 4, 1970, I celebrated my FIRST ANNIVERSARY, SOBER!!! What a night it was…my little brother and his fiancé, in the first row, Mom still sprinkling holy water on all, my sister who still needed a drink to get there, but was there, Jim and the folks from the Lodge, and of course, my sponsors, Ann and Audrey, and my fantastic Valley Stream Group! It was the joy of a lifetime and one of the highlights of my life. I am forever grateful for that night. In those days, the big thing, when you got your first year, was that the group gave you a cigarette lighter, as almost everyone smoked (hard to believe). My ZIPPO lighter with my sobriety date on it was the treasure of treasures. Of course, a few years later, as I was ruining my lungs and health from cigarettes, I had to quit.

However, my lighter remained a treasure until I passed it on to a smoker, someone I admired and loved.

Life was good. I enjoyed my two jobs…everyone there respected my sobriety and my work ethic. And with my new (to me) car, which I chose to call "Herby," made many meetings and took my close friends to meetings. I was upset that many of the women, I brought to the sessions, weren't staying sober! Then, my sponsors reminded me, "Yes, but Sue, YOU are staying sober, and that's what it's all about." Lesson learned.

One day, I had a call from a previous employer. They informed me that one of the accounts that I used to service, on Fifth Avenue, was looking for an Advertising Manager, and he thought it would be a great job for me. I panicked! Commuting by LIRR again, and I hadn't ridden the train sober yet! Oh my! I couldn't wait to run it by sponsors and my group family. All were excited for me and said, "YOU CAN DO IT!" I believed in and trusted them, and if they believed in me, then I had to try. A few of the guys, my brothers, offered to do a dry train run into the city with me to bolster my confidence...and they did, and it did! So, I applied and got the job! I was to be their first female advertising manager. What a new gift of sobriety! They said it would entail some business flights to the factory in Mass. But I had been honest with them about my past, and they always offered to watch out for me and also at any business parties I would attend. What a gift! And it worked out great! Then, my sponsors and group managed to help me grow and be blessed, and all were so proud and excited. My AA group became another family. And my own family was quite happy too!

February 7, 1970. It was a beautiful, sixty-degree summer day. My brother, Jimmy and his bride married and had a storybook wedding with a reception for about 150 people at a beautiful place in Long Island. As promised, I had my sponsors there and a few friends as well and was not one bit tempted when the champagne toast occurred. All went well, and it was a fairytale wedding in every respect.

We placed a little addendum here that my brother, being the only boy, was my mom's baby, and my sister and I were fine with it. Because of the age difference between him and my sister, he was like another son to her too. To me, he was my kid brother with a four-year age difference. We could fight over many things, but one thing was sure…we had each other's back and would attack anyone who tried to hurt either of us. For example, when he was six, and I was ten, we were out riding bikes. One boy, Curt, about twelve at the time, grabbed Jimmy and knocked him down, wanting his bike. Boy, was he ever sorry when Big Sister Sue, red pigtails and all, went soaring after him, knocked him down, and gave him a black eye!!! Motto: don't mess with the Boylston kids!!!

My sister, Joanne…

While my brother and I grew up together, my relationship with my sister, due to the 10-year age difference, took time to develop and grow. I was nine when she got married, ten, when she had her first child, and she often was like another mother at those ages. Years later, we got much closer and realized the grass looked greener on our opposite sides. I learned how she felt…so left out and alone… My brother and I had the same last name, which she wished my dad had given her. She had hoped he had adopted her. Ironically, my dad thought her family name as more prominent than his. He wanted her to keep that identity as much as he did want to adopt her. How sad, no one ever shared their reasoning, and when my sister learned that, it took the sting out of her loss. I loved her so and would always try to make it all up to her. She was able to see what looked great to her, in my life, wasn't that great after all. Then, I often stayed with her when her husband traveled, and we enjoyed her kids and a few drinks at night. She complained about her life. She envied my single, career girl lifestyle, and I saw her have what I hoped to have one day…husband and family…though I see, now, what I said and what I really wanted were two different things. As Joanne and I got closer, I began to trust her. I let her in on my double life in the city and shared my guilt and shame. She listened and tried to advise me, but I had a pretty closed mind, and now I can see how afraid I was of marriage and commitment. I constantly made choices of men who were unavailable. However, with the alcoholism creeping in, my mental and spiritual health was fast declining. Joanne drank with me and often alone. When I finally did get sober, she lost her drinking buddy, and worse yet, I couldn't spend much time with her as she was still drinking, and it bothered me. So, for the year of my sobriety, I lost my sister and felt bad about it. My brother and I knew that something was wrong with our sister but couldn't put our fingers on it. We never realized her drinking was progressing too.

In February 1971, Life was good again! I was sober for over a year, my career was going well, and my friend, Sally, and I often returned to the Lodge. There, we would speak and share our sobriety with the new people. I was scheduled to go up and speak on the weekend of February 13, but my mom was feeling very alone and didn't want me to go. I felt torn, but gave in and stayed home.

My brother and his wife went away to Vermont to celebrate their first wedding anniversary. He called to say, "So long!"

I told him to have a good time and, "Love you, brother!" Our family always ended every phone call with "Love you."

The next evening, tragedy struck, and my brother's wife, thinking I'm at the Lodge as planned, called the Lodge. Jim was the first to get the call that changed our lives forever. My sweet brother was killed by a drunk driver up in Vermont as he left the restaurant. His wife was a widow…and in shock!

Jim Cusack called me to offer condolences right after Maureen found me. I had to wake up Mom and tell her the worst news any mother ever had to hear. We were all devastated, nowhere to go, how to wrap our heads around this…we couldn't… My sponsors and the Twelve Steps group were around us the next day like flies…they never let go, and thank God for them. The blessing was we were able to have an open-casket since the accident was quite bad, they weren't sure. We wanted to see him one more time, and we did. It was hard to believe. I shook with nerves. I didn't want a drink but did wish I could have a Valium to calm my nerves. Luckily, I talked about it; about how whoever killed my brother would have to live with this the rest of his life – two families shattered forever. Our program taught us to accept the things we cannot change, and at that moment, I had to lean on every person and everything I was ever taught. My Twelve Step group was there for us all. My sister came down the night we heard, and I learned that she tied her foot to mine when we tried to sleep as even though she was still drinking, she was trying to make sure I didn't. That was one gift in all this already – my big sister protecting me from myself; she really liked me being sober and wanted to help me. That meant the world to me amidst all this grief and pain.

We got through the funeral, and while others were buying Valentine flowers, we were buying my brother's funeral flowers. It was painful; truly a nightmare! After the funeral, everyone went home. There was no luncheon, no friends-and-family. Somehow, we were too much in shock to plan, and there wasn't much real family. Not knowing what else to do, I took my mom to my group and meetings every night. We shared what happened, to prevent anyone else, who drank and drove, from going down this road. We were with people who cared, and they kept us busy and loved.

As time went on, Mom and I had trouble living in the old house we had lived in for so many years. Taxes and expenses were mounting, repairs were beyond our means, and resultantly, it was time to sell. We hoped it would give us a fresh start, and with my salary, we figured we could afford a rent of $250 per month. We found a lovely two-family house renting the main floor, and we took it. Once again, my Twelve Steps group brothers came through, helped us move, and we began our new life in Valley Stream. My brother's wife went through various stages of grieving alone, and then with us, and we all kept close.

A Gift in this Tragedy

One Saturday morning, about six months after Jimmy's death, my sister called me for help. She said, "Your program advises to call for help, so here I am. Just take me to a hotel for the weekend, and don't let me drink." So, of course, I told her that's not how it works. I suggested we make a reservation at the Lodge, where I went, and she agreed!!! However, she wanted me to tell the Director, Jim, that she wanted a crash course of two weeks to be ready for her son's wedding in January. And she would do the ashtray chore; no dishes or cooking.

We put in the request, and the miracle began. It went on for thirty, beautiful years: a sober mom at her son's wedding, and years later, a sober Grandma, and an inspiration to us all.

But here I have jumped ahead… I called Jim at the Lodge to see if he would help my sister, and of course, he said yes. We'll talk about her "crash course" treatment plan later. When I drove into the Lodge, many were concerned it was me coming back after the loss of my brother. But thank God and the program, I managed to get the day off from work and drive my sister to Jim. As I came in, Jim looked at me with a look of care and concern and maybe admiration that I had never seen before. He had become a good friend by then, but there was something more that day…something I appreciated like a mutual caring and respect. Prior to that, he had become one of the first male friends I ever had with no angles. He was respectful and kind to all of us, and he would do anything to save another alcoholic. He was the sole counselor at the Lodge and managed to help all of us get honest and on track with sobriety. He told me I was pretty sick and had no more chances, and it's good I believed him.

Now, we all know that Jim became the love of my life: soul mate, best friend, husband – my ALL. So, how did it all happen? All I can say is that it was something beyond us. They say that, "God writes straight with crooked lines," and so, this is how we came to pass.

Jim did his magic with my sister in two weeks... Everyone held their breath as they thought she was only doing it to be sober for her son's wedding, and then crash after that. Jim, in his wisdom, advised giving her benefit of the doubt. He said that it was OK to take her to my group and introduce her to other women. My sponsors were criticizing me for taking her around at first, but once she got to know people, she did get her own sponsor and worked her own program. So, while I lost my brother that year, I gained my sister back and was blessed to have her for many years to come.

Joanne went home in October, stayed sober, and her son, my first nephew, had a lavish storybook wedding on Long Island in January. Our whole family was still grieving my brother, and we knew it would be a tough one. But, then, my sister and I were allies again and had each other.

My first nephew was my sister's baby and only nineteen. So, it wasn't very easy for her to accept it all. He married into a large family, and they planned to have over 300 guests, with both a Rabbi and Priest perform the ceremony. It all went off smoothly, and the bride and groom went off to live in Virginia and continue college and graduate school. Joanne, then, could concentrate on her daughter, who was going away to college, and with the help of the program, stay sober through the years to come. She did, and Jim was very happy for us all.

Back to me, I was then sober for about a year and a half. My sponsors pushed me into serving on the big Dinner Dance Committee at the Hilton in October, honoring Bill

Wilson, our founder of Alcoholics Anonymous. I was one of the hosts. Hundreds of people were expected, and I was nervous, not happy about it, but doing what was suggested. The date was October 9, 1971. Something happened that night that was a part of the plan. As I stood and greeted, Jim and his group from the Lodge appeared and went to their table. Jim came over to me later, and asked if he could see me for a cup of coffee. He had coffee and apple pie, I had coffee and a cigarette. He told me he had feelings for me that were pretty serious, that he felt he was in love with me, and that under the circumstances, we should not continue my speaking commitments at the Lodge. He said that he thought too much of me to not address it and simply pull away. I said I understood as I was feeling the same way and didn't know how and if I should pull away. So, it was a bittersweet night, and on top of it, was our treasured Founder, Bill Wilson's last big appearance. He was very ill with emphysema and COPD (chronic obstructive pulmonary disease).

I went home and told my mother, and that I was thinking of us moving to California. I knew my feelings for Jim had become deeper than I wanted to admit. He was a genuinely kind and caring man and without wanting to, I had fallen in love with him. But it all seemed wrong so much was at stake: his marriage, stepchildren; who did know and love me, the Lodge.

Having been in a situation like this before, I knew it couldn't ever go the same way…no secrets, lying, or cheating. Somehow, if it was meant to be, it had to be right, and true, and above all, include God in it.

I had found my way back to my Catholic faith via passing and going to St. Francis church on Thirty-first Street. I loved going to communion every day. Jim knew this and shared that he missed communion since his last two marriages were out of the church.

I had a priest confessor there, Fr. Phillip, and I took him into my confidence about Jim. I also spoke to another priest, that my mom and I were close to, in Far Rockaway, who helped us through my brother's death. Both of them felt they would like to meet Jim, and said I shouldn't run away from it.

We had no cell phones in those days. Thus, a conversation with Jim was scarce and probably for the best. However, when I told Jim that Fr. Murphy in Far Rockaway suggested they talk, he went right down to see him. I thought that was pretty caring. He later told me he thought the priest had a crush on me and wanted to check him out! Fr. Murphy did help Jim with the fact that he still could go to communion, no one could stop him, and it was between him and God. So, Jim went back to communion on his own and prayed long and hard.

God writes straight with crooked lines?? Now, what after a long a painful time for all, and not seeing each other for months? Just a few phone calls here and there, Jim faced everyone and everything. He did what he had to and left the Lodge and all behind. On May 4, 1972, I felt such guilt and pain but talked it over often and faced it with both sponsors and priests. We also made a vow we would not live together or be intimate until we could marry.

He went out to stay with his brother, and we finally could date, no matter how many (and they did) turned against us, we were lucky to have a few true friends who stuck by us. My mom, sister, and family were there... Jim's sister-in-law, who was always there for him, his brother, and a few Twelve Steps friends.

We stayed sober, and Jim had to overcome being black-balled in the field for several months. Monsignor Dunne of the NYPD turned against Jim, and wouldn't help him. Unbeknownst to us, my mother wrote quite a scathing letter to the Monsignor. She told him he had no right to condemn Jim as he stood up and did the honest and right thing when many of the Monsignor's own men were drinking and cheating on their wives left and right. What was he doing to them? It must have worked because shortly after, Monsignor called Jim and recommended him to start the program for the Sisters up in Monticello. It was the beginning of Veritas Villa in 1973.

Prior to the above, I was still working at my job as Advertising Manager on Fifth Avenue. Jim would come in and take me to lunch and meet the President of the company, as they had all heard about him from me. My boss, the President, loved Jim and was happy for me. While Jim was in limbo with the job he loved, of helping alcoholics, he got a great job at an Insurance Co. and became one of their top sales managers!

We all know Jim can sell anyone anything, which is why he was extremely good at helping people stay sober. We went to Mass often, took many trips to Jim's favorite shrine in Auriesville, NY, and prayed for Jim to find his way back to his mission and a life as husband and wife.

One day Jim's brother told him about a divorce and marriage possibility in Haiti. After much research and apprehensive planning, we had the first destination wedding in our family. Jim and I flew down first and booked two rooms at the beautiful Ibolele Hotel in Porto Prince.

Papa Doc was ruling the country then, and things were not too welcoming for tourists. Our Haitian Tour guide arranged all as we had to stay seven days, get a license, and blood work in this very strange country. While I had wanted two separate rooms until we were married, the sounds of voodoo drums constantly in the mountains, and a black cat on the porch of our hotel changed my mind. I was petrified and settled for two separate beds to be safe. Everything was strange and scary, but we were so in love and willing to "march into hell" for our Impossible Dream and heavenly cause of marrying and beginning our life together. And so, on August 7, 1972, we were married in St. Yves Catholic church in Haiti with my mom, sister, and sister-in-law present. At last, we could begin our lives together, so much in love and ready to follow God's plan for our lives.

Now, we must introduce Jim's mom.

She and his dad were happy he had found the Lodge and was kind of settled up there. However, they didn't like the fact that he left his faith and were always praying behind the scenes, that he finds his way back to the church. We are not saying this was the end…all be all…and they were right… BUT they prayed some pretty serious prayers to get Jim back to the church! So, he did get there…fell in love with me, who fell back in love with my church and communion! There are those crooked lines. So, Jim's dad died in 1970 and didn't know about Jim's future, but was fairly content with him helping people, especially when Jim was helping priests who drank.

Jim's mom and I had a great rapport before Jim left the Lodge, but was very angry and upset afterward, and wouldn't talk to us for over a year. We could understand as she was embarrassed and had her own rapport with his ex-wife and stepchildren, but we kept trying to include her in our life. It finally worked, and she forgave us and made it easier for Jim's family to include us all.

Over the years, we made peace with Jim's ex-wife and even took her youngest boy to live with us when he turned sixteen as he needed Jim in his life.

Love conquers all, and patience is the virtue that helps, and it did.

We were married about a year when Jim's prayers to return to his calling of helping alcoholics received two answers. First, the letter from my mom to Monsignor finally showed results, as the Monsignor invited Jim to some meetings. He recommended Jim to go up to St. Josephs in Monticello, NY, and help them begin an addiction treatment program. Jim went up for the interview while I was at work in the city.

He loved the place! He told me it had such potential with great buildings and grounds he couldn't wait to show me. I was extremely happy for him being so happy and pictured a beautiful hotel setting in the mountains. It was far from that, but Jim was a visionary, and we knew we could make a go of it. I believed in him and was ready to do more than just make money. We were going to follow a mission, with God as our partner and give people help and hope to recover. The nuns would provide us with a building, freezer full of food, and phone, and the rest was in God's hands.

Ironically, the next day, Jim was offered an ideal comfy city job, and he was torn...only for a few hours...as he thought it would be best for me. Deep down, I knew his heart was already in the mountains of Monticello, and his first commitment was to the nuns. So, we both agreed to go for it, after much anguish and letter writing to each other.

We opened Veritas Villa on Memorial Day in May 1973. We began with a picnic backed by 400 recovered New York City policemen with their families who were ordered to go to the opening day picnic. It kicked us off, putting Jim back at the helm. The old nuns, who were going to put bars on their windows for the alcoholics, loved the nice young cops and their families and were going to pray for us every day.

Now, I share Jim's and my marriage, and the love we shared with God and each other. Here comes our "Impossible Dream."

We were married for one year when we packed up everything and moved to the mountains and our new adventure. Both our employers were very happy for us and said if it didn't work out, we could come back. They admired us following our dreams. We were very much in love and still happy to be sharing our mission... Jim following his calling to help alcoholics and me helping him. How true it is in the giving we receive as I found my deepest love in helping other alcoholics, especially recognizing women's needs in recovery.

Jim promised to take me out of the "rat race" of NYC and the working and commuting of Long Island. However, it wasn't long before I found myself in a lovely country farmhouse overrun with mice! City girl in the country…trying to impress my family…how happy I was…learning how to cope with mice, bats, bugs, and all sorts of country living. We quickly adopted a neighbor's kitten, who grew into our mouse warrior and kept us mouse free, except for the one or two he would leave us as gifts on our bed as a token of his love for us. Oh yes, I loved Jim and our mission dearly, but this was a whole new world! I worked late as we developed the program at the Villa rather than go home alone.

Our agreement with the Sisters was that we would work without compensation until we began getting the accounts back and up and running.

Thanks to Monsignor and his 400 NYC policemen! They arrived for our first picnic and put Jim on the map again. Jim received his first paycheck in September. I agreed to wait a year before going on a salary. To compensate for our income, I went to work for a local newspaper in Monticello, enjoying using my advertising skills. The owners gave me a page to write every week under the name, "Suzy Cu." I interviewed every business I could find in Monticello, many of whom were restaurants. So, Jim and I enjoyed many complimentary dinners and got to know all our new neighbors.

In between, I was secretary to my Jim, helped develop the program as we know it today, and worked with the families on weekends. My favorite job was often, but not always, sitting with Jim as he performed his magic on every client. If it was a woman, he had me there to accompany him as he helped her admit to, and deal with, her addiction problem. He adapted himself to each group he ran. He skillfully carved his way around their denial, zeroed in on

44

one person, and got them to open up to where he was taking them. It was an art to watch… I called him Surgeon of the Soul as he had a gift to reach the soul and the heart of each person. If he had to be tough and tear them open, he always, like a gifted surgeon, put them together again. They left him feeling loved and cared for, no matter what he did. On weekends, we enjoyed our family work. Distraught wives, scared children, hopeless husbands, all visited, and between Jim and I, each family was seen individually. In the beginning, I accompanied Jim and watched how he worked. His first question to the family member was always, "How do you think he/she is doing?" It was his key question as the response told him everything. If they quickly answered, "Good" or "I see a big change," he knew we were on the right track.

If they hesitated, we knew we had more work to do on that client. It could be either chipping away at the denial or tackling the many troubling issues that came along with each person's addiction.

Subconsciously, I learned so much from Jim and began utilizing it with my own style in counseling women. We became tired of trying to prevent the men and women from getting emotionally involved while in treatment. We finally recognized that the "attraction addiction" between two emotionally ill alcoholics was just as dangerous as drinking, and so developed two separate programs. It took time, and years later, more staff, to implement them. But I learned and believed that it was a part of my purpose in our dream. Jim always listened intently to my inner voice and was my best cheerleader of women's needs. We thank Jim for our women's only program; by women, for women.

Back then, Jim and I were the only staff at the time, and helping alcoholics was a new field. We were yet to be part of a group that developed a Credential for Alcoholism Counselors. Jim was asked by the State of New York to help organize what we know as OASAS today, and he helped develop the first Credential, attaining Number 15. I later applied, was given, and still hold Number 86! We are very proud of those credentials, and I feel proud that Jim was one of the founders!

We were there for about a year, and the Sisters visited and asked how they could help. Jim said to them, "Just sit and talk to the clients, you'll see." And they did. They were fascinated at how effective their kindness, interest, and compassion were in helping those in our care. NYC police were overwhelmed that two Sisters cared about them and their addiction.

At the same time, a new course was being given in NYC, twice a week, by Monsignor, Chaplain of the NYCPD, and his group NYC ACCEPT (Alcoholism Counseling Course). The two Sisters and I attended and received our certificates. Both sisters felt they could be even more effective if they continued to attain their Social Work degrees (which they did) and returned to teach and counsel.

Years went by, and I learned to love the country and adapt to the continuous snow from October 'til April (one Easter we actually had snow up there).

Circa 1979... Our Icelandic Guests

Iceland was having an epidemic of alcoholism, affecting the professionals, judiciaries, and everyone else. Somehow, a prominent judge found his way to a hospital on Long Island, and then to the Villa and Jim Cusack for a month. He went back home and became the role model for sobriety. As a result, the Icelandic government set up a fund to offer the magic of the hospital and the Villa to ALL their alcoholics seeking help.

It went on successfully for over eight years until they set up their own programs back in Iceland.

During the years of offering treatment to our Icelandic friends, many funny stories occurred as we grew together. One day, we had a call from our Villa neighbor, the House of Prayer, then housing nuns on retreat.

"Mr. Cusack, we have a problem! There is a group of nude sunbathers on the top of an old truck behind our building. Will you please check it out!"

Of course, it was our "ecstatic need to find sunlight." Icelandic guests...innocently soaking up rays of the sun that were like gold to them...In Iceland, there can be months of darkness and very little sun.

We explained it was a bit of a problem in the nude, and all was changed to sunbathing with clothing!

After years of using the language of the heart to share experience, strength, and hope via translators, thousands of Icelanders found sobriety and brought it back to Iceland.

If any of you are still out there and remember these days, please reach out to us.

P.S. Clothing was so expensive in Iceland that a supervised shopping trip to buy jeans etc. was part of the treatment plan!

I was always very close to my mother and sister and missed them when we moved. Jim, being the special husband and FRIEND, was grateful for my upstate move. He developed a surprise plan for me. Once a month, he would plan a day on Long Island, so I could hang out with my mom and sister. He joined a gym as he wanted to keep trim and loved working out. We all met for dinner before heading back up to Monticello! Once Jim's mother forgave us for falling in love and marrying, we visited her in Middle Village on the way home. It was a win-win-win! That was my Jim.

We were happy, loved each other, and prayed that we be blessed with our own little baby. We made many trips to the Auriesville Shrine that had brought us this far and waited.

One day it happened! The signs were all there. We went to the doctor and had him confirm the magic words, "You are going to have a baby!!!" We cried tears of joy: Jim was then forty-four, and I was thirty-two…first child for us both…so, we were both happy and then frightened with the overwhelming responsibility of it all. My mother was a bit reserved with her joy, and at that moment, I couldn't figure out why (later I realized she was still concerned about my dad and herself having been third cousins, but she kept it to herself).

Jim's mom and everyone else were all thrilled and happy for us. The Villa and the nuns were excited for the new life coming and the success of the entire Villa venture.

I was so proud and excited to be a Mother… something I always hoped for but never dreamed possible. Time went by, and the excitement and our love for each other and our new baby grew. We drove to Auriesville to thank God for this special gift.

Three months of utter joy and anticipation ended cruelly and abruptly when we suffered a miscarriage. I say "we" because many times, people overlook the pain and loss the father suffers. Jim and I were devastated. Dreams of infants, sharing, and raising a child with all the excitement were gone in an instant. Jim was worried about my health, as his first wife had suffered a miscarriage, and never fully recovered. She died a few years later at the age of twenty-six. I blamed myself for doing too much or not enough… We were both full of pain and sorrow, and consoled each other as best as we could. For better or worse, those marriage vows took on a deeper meaning for us both. We leaned on our family and friends, and especially, a small couples' group we had gathered. Over a period of ten years, we carried each other through life on life's terms. We helped each other through everything imaginable and were a tremendous help at this time.

Unfortunately, when a miscarriage occurs, people don't really know what to say. I suffered through family gatherings with comments like, "you'll have another" or "you can have one of mine."

The years went by, and while we kept hoping, it just never happened. I often felt I let Jim down and there was something wrong with me, he felt the same, then we tried to adopt children, and nothing worked. Through it all, we continued helping all the alcoholics and addicts who came to our doors and got lost in our special mission. Finally, many years later, we came to see that God gave us so much, but we were never to have our own biological children. It was a loss we shared and learned to accept as we became the instruments to help all our "kids" at the Villa become the parents and grandparents they should be. We also shared in the lives of all our nieces and nephews and step-children from Jim's previous families. They were as close to being our own in the love and time we shared with them.

Eight years at the Villa in Monticello went by, and one day, we were hit by devastating news… While the Villa was very successful, it only accounted for a few acres of property the nuns owned. There was another property, of 1500 acres, which was not holding on its own. They were forced to sell it to a developer. They had hoped to give us 30 acres on which to keep the Villa, but it wasn't meant to be.

So here we were… Jim at fifty-one and I at thirty-nine…having to find a home for thirty retired residents we had acquired over the years, a staff of eight, a husky dog, Totem, who we adored, a cat who really kept the mice away, and ourselves.

We began to spread the word that we needed a place. All our friends started suggesting ideas to help. Ironically, we attended a conference in Austin, Texas, in June of that year, 1981. There, we met a New York neighbor who happened to own a beautiful piece of property in downstate, NY. He wanted to utilize it for addiction recovery and envisioned a treatment center. Of course, once he and Jim began to talk, it looked like the perfect fit. As soon as we went home, we got together, and our new friend showed us his beautiful property. It was on the top of a mountain that had once been known as a Winery. There was a pretty house on the property, which could be ours and in time, Jim and I, along with the couple who owned it thought we could all partner and make it happen. It was agreed we would hire lawyers, take it to our accounts and the town board for approval and go from there. It sounded like an answer to our prayers and a dream come true. Even though Jim wasn't too keen on having a partner, our options weren't too great.

The first negative sign I received was one that I didn't want to talk about or recognize, as I really wanted this to work. When I spotted the large dead bird on the floor of the fireplace in the pretty house, I pretended it wasn't there. I didn't want to upset Jim and was truly hoping this place would be the answer to our prayers. But in my gut, I knew this wasn't right. I was raised that birds of any kind, dead or alive when INSIDE the house meant bad luck. I wish I could erase it, but when you are raised with these things, and death and sickness appear along with the birds, it's hard to overlook. However, I did, and we continued with our plan. All through the summer, we met, and by August, we had to meet with the town board. All havoc broke loose as half the town showed up to keep us out!!! A week later, someone had cruelly beaten and injured one of the winery owners' treasured dogs. Could we have fought it…yes…but did we want to put everyone in danger… absolutely not! Thus, after heartbreaking decisions (much to my relief as my bird sign had warned me), we walked away from the partnership, and vowed to pray and keep in touch.

We were close to September, and the new owners of St. Josephs wanted us out by October!!!

We were back to square one to find a new home.

Our mothers, families, and friends were anxious. We prayed.

We had saved only a few thousand dollars. We borrowed all we could and mustered up a down payment for some big building somewhere…we knew not where!

Off to our only place we went in good times and in bad times…Auriesville Shrine…to pray for a new home and some quick direction.

It had to be the prayers because the night we arrived home, a real estate man we had asked to help us called with just what he thought we could use. It was a two-story hotel in Kerhonkson, NY, owned by a drug facility. They wanted to move to California, and we needed a home quickly. Our lawyer and real estate man got it together, and after many meetings, we had a deal. Low down payment with two mortgage payments and balloon payments. I was so excited and told Jim not to worry…he could do it…I believed in him and his expertise. I didn't worry too well by Jim's standards in those days…faith and holy water would get us through.

One of the older nuns, Sr. Poly, loved Jim and the work we did and left Jim a message not to worry…All would work out. I sure believed her.

On the day of the closing on our new home (hotel), we were all set when we were hit with a snag…names were not right on the papers. I got out the Auriesville holy water, sprinkled it all around, and within an hour, it all went through!!! The time it went through was 2:00 p.m. We found out later that day that our buddy Sr. Poly died at precisely 2:00 p.m. on the same day…on October 9, 1981.

Was it a coincidence, or did she go straight to heaven and make it happen? Our lawyer and real estate man wanted bottles of that holy water for their next deals!

And so, on October 10, 1981, we moved the Villa program, seamlessly and without missing a group, along with all the people involved, into our new home.

Jim's business expertise prevailed, and before long, the Villa was flourishing. We added many staff members and trained them all in Jim's philosophy of family-style treatment...combining love, respect, and discipline in conjunction with the Twelve Steps.

In 1982, we finally were able to give our mom's the peace of knowing we had our own place and wanted to make their lives easier. We thought of taking them on trips and many good things.

Unfortunately, God had other plans. My beloved mom, one of our best friends, became very ill and was in hospital for weeks. All she wanted was to come up to us in the country and be with us. Her best friend, John, who she had met in the Senior Citizen's group, and fell in love with, wanted to come up and help. We had since adopted him as our dad, and Jim and I double-dated with them often. Every time we attempted to get her out of the hospital, she had a setback. Finally, knowing her time was limited, we asked if we could get an ambulance and bring her up to our home and care for her there. Jim told her it would happen...she knew if he said then it would. We had it all set up, but that morning, just as we all came into her room in the hospital, once we were all there, she passed away. What a heartbreak...but the consolation was ... she knew we wanted her upstate...she knew we were taking her home and died knowing that. As my heart broke, that fact and Jim's love got me through my next big loss. She died near Mother's Day that year, and we were in the funeral home on Mother's Day.

We went home to carry on the Villa mission and also had moved Jim's mom up to live with us. She kept me busy in between times, and while she was a tough Irish mom, we had a great rapport, and I always remembered I wouldn't have Jim without her!

She and Jim always had a tough relationship, both having strong wills, but it had softened over the years. Her heart, too, was failing and was often in and out of the hospital near us. In September of this same year, Jim was heading out to attend a men's retreat and told me he was going to go have breakfast with his mom before he left. It was a nice surprise for his mom and when he went, he said it was the best talk and moments he'd had in a long time with her. She even told him, "…You know, Jimmy, you really weren't that bad!" They said that they loved each other and hugged goodbye. An hour later, she passed away. When I called Jim, he was sad but said he had a strange peace that overcame him and was able to go out and break the news to his brother. Thus, we lost the two people who never gave up on us, who prayed thousands of rosaries…our mothers and best friends left us in the same year …1982.

We were grateful we did all we could with them but had wanted more time…we always do…and then, we had each other and our siblings. We went on to treasure them and be with them as much as we could.

Life seemed to be good for most of us in the late '80s early '90s. The Villa flourished and was able to help hundreds. Jim would often keep people on for months until he felt they were well enough to leave. He had a reputation for being tough on the disease but kind to the people, and had a huge heart for helping anyone, anywhere.

We would be running out the door to a family wedding, and he would spot one guy being nasty to his wife…make him sit right down and keep him another month. He was truly unique in his field, and I was blessed to share him with everyone.

During those good years, we began to travel and focus on staying healthy and found a beautiful small home in Hilton Head, South Carolina. We bought if from an elderly couple in their '80s who had loved it for years and wanted it to go to another couple whose family would enjoy it. It was the third-row ocean and for thirty years became the favorite paradise getaway for all our siblings, cousins, friends, and relatives. Jim loved sports, and we bought each other bikes for Valentine's Day in 1986. We rode the beach and bike paths for miles. It was a great place to find peace and rejuvenate ourselves for the intense work we did at the Villa. It truly was heaven on earth, and we enjoyed it as long as we possibly could. Our family members had their children take their first steps there…our logbook recorded every treasured memory.

One day, while driving home from Hilton Head around the year 1992, Jim had to pull over as he felt a shade had come down on one eye, and he couldn't see. It was the beginning of his ongoing eye problems that were to plague him. We were told it was his optic nerve, and that part of it was damaged. We went all over to doctors; many said it was permanent, and there was no reason why it happened. We prayed a lot, and by some miracle were led to the help of a dear friend, Peter, who introduced us to a psychiatrist. Dr. Gerald was skilled in the healing power of visionary and imaging techniques and had cured Peter's cancer. The psychiatrist was an amazing spiritual man who helped people use the power of their own mind to improve, and in some cases, heal their illnesses. Jim and I met with him and felt something special and hopeful, and we wanted to try anything to help Jim's sight. After about a year of seeing him once a month, and using the mental imaging he personalized for Jim to use daily, his eyesight improved! The optic nerve had healed …even the doctors couldn't explain how or why!

Shortly after, Dr. Gerald contacted Jim to check if he agreed to appear on a famous TV Show, along with another of his patients, and testify to the "power of the mind" and their work together. They were also cautioned there would be a few people on the show who would try to attack and de-bunk the credibility of the doctor and his patients. Jim loved a good controversy, especially since he was so grateful to prove how much Dr. Gerald had helped him. To this day, I am amazed how well and professionally Jim controlled himself. He and his eye recovery underwent attacks from an attorney and another doctor. But, at the end, one left the show with a lot of hope and mental space to draw one's own conclusion (I still have a video of the show I watch when I remember that day). As for Jim and me, we basked in the miracle Jim was given, as on that very day, he had driven us down from upstate to the city!!! He managed well for many years until other cataract problems occurred that were more the results of a surgery that went wrong.

Jim's eyesight was an ongoing problem, and a cross Jim had to bear it. However, he did it bravely and rarely complained.

Jim was often called "Apple eyes" when he was a kid. And as an adult, he had these beautiful big blue eyes which everyone loved, but those big eyes were a problem when having to have surgeries, etc. In addition to the optic nerve he had earlier, he developed an early cataract which required to be taken out. This was before all the new technology, so he had to wear special glasses. Then came years of another cataract and an attempt to insert the lens. But his eyes were so big they never took the lens properly. Over the years, as his eyes became worse, he and I learned to compensate. I did all the driving, and we held hands often, which we loved to do anyway, even while walking around. By the year 2000, biking was no longer something we could do, but hiking and walking the beach was something he could handle. During all this time, he was still running groups, counseling, and was able to see a lot of things in our clients that no one else did. He had a sixth sense about treatment and could spot 'B.S.' a mile away.

Around the mid '90s, our accounts wanted us to open an outpatient facility in the city. We bought a floor in a building on Madison Avenue and hired a couple to run it for us. My gut feeling was never positive about this idea, but not wanting to put a damper on the Villa's progress, I went along and never shared my feelings with Jim. Two years later, it went sour, and he wished I had told him, but at least we tried it and were able to sell it and come out. It just wasn't our forte. Inpatient is us; outpatient is another ballgame and not us. The only good thing was that to attend meetings and be part of the outpatient, we purchased a cute but small apartment on Central Park South right near the theaters and restaurants. Both of us and our families enjoyed many shows and good times together over the years.

Slowly, we noticed that Jim was out of breath very easily and having a tough time walking around. This was in 1996, and we were told he had a seriously damaged mitral valve that needed to be replaced. Back then, they weren't as easily repaired as now, and we were both full of fear and apprehension. We were sent to Dr. Wayne, who operated on many celebrities successfully and had to wait two months to see him, and then another month for surgery in the city. I'll never forget the day we both left the Villa for the hospital…we had listened to many tapes before on positive heart surgery, and yet we both knew this could go either way. We had been to our Auriesville shrine and turned it over. Our sisters-in-law and brothers-in-law were all there for us and me when Jim went into surgery. I gave the doctor a bottle of Auriesville holy water and asked him if he could leave it in surgery with him. He humbly and graciously popped it into his pocket and was glad to have it. Midway through surgery, he said all was going as planned, and he was about to place a St. Jude Mitral valve in Jim's heart.

I was pleased it had a Saint on it but realized later it was made in the town of St. Jude. Anyway…it all sure worked as nine hours later, Jim was in recovery and the next day able to sit up and talk. It was a long but successful recovery, and we were able to stay in our apartment to be close to the doctor. At the picnic that year, it was a gift to see Jim strong and able to work out and walk around. That valve and all the prayers gave him to me, our loved ones, the Villa, and the people needing help for another twenty years! I must remember this when I mourn him now…what a blessing that doctor, that valve, and all those prayers were! An extra twenty years!!!

You may recall that I had a gut feeling about purchasing and developing that Villa Outpatient Center on Madison Avenue. I always loved the city and still often missed the excitement and magic it held. Jim knew this and was happy he could give me a bit of the city back in our lives this way. But the work we did there went against the grain with me. We had hired a couple, as equal partners, to help us run the facility, but about six months into the venture, we knew it was not working out. Our work ethics weren't compatible, and the financial part fell entirely on us. Worse yet, I had trouble with people showing up drunk, angry, and not really wanting to be there, yet we were profiting from their attendance. Whether we were able to help them or not, their treatment could go on, and it was all about them getting a letter for court or whatever. At the end of the first year, I had developed severe bowel problems, and both Jim and I were discouraged with the Villa Outpatient.

Then, it was my turn to face serious surgery…a colon resection and outcome based on what the surgeon would find during the operation. We were led to an excellent doctor at NYC, and I was blessed to have had a successful resection… no cancer and no colostomy needed. I was in the hospital for seven days, and Jim never left my side. His love and encouragement kept me going, and we were lucky to have our apartment in the city to go "home" to and heal. One of the things I loved about Jim was that no matter how important he was at work or anywhere else, he always put me first. Whenever I needed him, without even my asking, he was THERE. He was also such a great listener and comfort-giver, and I was blessed with this soul mate who got me through so many things…especially this.

By then, we both knew it was time to dissolve the partnership, which had turned bitter. Our lawyer at the time finally told us he would handle it, as Jim was losing patience and his cool as well. Once the partnership was over, and we were totally responsible for the ownership, we were able to place the business on the market.

Within six months, we were blessed to find a couple, just like us, who had a dream to own their own outpatient and willing to go to any lengths to make it happen. We barely broke even with the final sale price but were relieved to be free of the entire responsibility. Then, we were able to go back home to Kerhonkson and concentrate solely on what we loved and were meant to do…our inpatient "baby" …the Villa. It had suffered along the way, too, with a lot of our wrong choices. It's important here I share we learned some invaluable lessons for ourselves.

To thine own selves be true…sometimes we do the right things for the wrong reasons, and in trying to please others, lose ourselves. All business owners learn by trial and error and become better for it. Jim always would say to someone making decisions…there is no right or wrong decision…there is only the HONEST DECISION.

If it was an honest decision, we could live with the outcome of it. There, we came to the honest decision that strengthened our marriage, our business, our lives, and lives of those all around us. We were glad we had tried something new, but were able to admit it wasn't for us and let it go.

During these years, too, we kept thinking that to perpetuate the Villa, we had to find some bigger and better place than us to merge, partner or give it to. We felt we weren't smart enough to perpetuate it as our own Foundation and that larger and more corporate type treatment centers would know better what to do to. After much trial and error, and getting to know many of the leaders of those places, all said we should keep on doing what we were doing and not change. They felt Jim had created his vision in a unique way…developed a philosophy based on family love and fellowship, that bigger business and corporate type centers would ruin. Our love for each other grew during these years as we learned and explored our business ventures together.

During this time too, we were successful financially and were able to share trips and good times with our families. Beyond our wildest dreams, both grateful and sober a number of years, we were blessed to enjoy sections each year of World Cruises on the Queen Elizabeth II. Our sisters and brothers-in-law, who were our friends as well all along traveled to China, Japan, Canary Islands, and were blessed with more than we ever imagined. The best part of it all was, we always looked forward to returning home to Kerhonkson, doing what we loved best with the ones we loved at the Villa.

Nothing lasts forever, and health issues and aging begin to affect all our traveling buddies, one by one cruelly. The first was my dear friend and sister, who stayed sober all these years with me… even worked with me in our women's unit for about a year and was truly a best friend. We had all smoked, but she had gone on longer than I could and developed COPD. It hit her slowly and insidiously. It slowed her down and seriously affected her and all the fun things we did. With her grandchildren… traveling…trips in the summer to Saratoga Race Track … all of us enjoying the races…and the magic of Saratoga in the Summer.

We managed to do everything we could anyway. I hung out with her as we sent the guys to the top of Mount Everest by cable car, or to Masada in Jerusalem. We helped her cope as she had more problems catching her breath. My heart would break for her, and Jim began helping as well since he was doing pretty good after his heart surgery.

A few years more, and we endured the heartbreak of watching my sister slowly deteriorate as she added oxygen to help her breathe and move around a little better.

I remember her crying and us running down to meet my brother-in-law and her right after her doctor gave her the news that she needed oxygen 24/7. It was like we all received a death sentence even though we tried to make it all palatable. We planned to have oxygen when she visited us…have it on the ships when we sailed…rent a van and travel with it to Hilton Head and Saratoga… and we did. But nothing was ever the same. We would eat out always with an eye towards easy access in and out and where was the ladies' room so Joanne could get there easily enough. As it got tougher for her to get around, we added a portable wheelchair to the mix, and all took turns pushing her along with us. But our love for each other kept us going and kept Joanne with us …feeling wanted and loved, and we made the most of whatever time we had. I remember reading books and checking articles on end-stage COPD, and crying when I realized we were getting close. My sister had such courage… she kept us all going, and rarely complained. Since we had already lost our brother, we especially treasured our friendship and time together.

One summer day, we were heading up to Saratoga for opening day…Joanne loved it and didn't care how bad she felt… we were going. I'll never forget that day. We wheeled her to our beautiful table on the finish line, greeting all our friends around us on this big day. She was having a bit of a tough time, but gave me her choice of horses in the first race, and off we were. Jim had picked a few winners he thought could do it, so we followed and were all set. We won the first race, but suddenly Joan's breathing became worse. We knew something was wrong. I called our local doctor, Dr. John, who asked us to bring her from Saratoga to his office immediately. Her oxygen level was so low that they had to airlift her to Westchester Medical, and the nightmare began. Suddenly, life was out of our hands…she was taken away by helicopter, and none of us could go with her. My poor brother-in-law was in shock.

Joanne was intubated and saved, but it is a grueling thing to watch a loved one who's had it. They can see and hear but can't talk. You see the fear in their eyes, and you try to be aware they depend on you for their reality. It's a nightmare. Jim, Joanne's husband, and I stayed in a hotel nearby for the entire month…one of us always with her…they finally managed to get her off the ventilator, but things were not good. We took her home to our house in Kerhonkson as I could help care for her, and we could be there as well. Jim was wonderful and there for us all as always. We were so blessed he was well and grateful to help.

Joanne celebrated her seventieth birthday at our home with catering a cake, and her kids and grandkids right there. Shortly after, she wanted to go back to her home in Long Island to be near her kids. She was home a week and ended back up in Winthrop Hospital, unable to breathe, with the only option of placing her back on a Ventilator (intubated again). She called us aside and said she could not take that and wanted hospice care. She bravely said she was ready to let go, and she begged us to accept this. She wanted the grandkids then twelve and ten to come in and say goodbye. Her courage was astounding, and to this day, I cry writing about it…she told me how much she loved me, and that…me, the little sister had become the big sister…for which she was so grateful. I asked her if through all this, she ever thought of having a drink. She said, "absolutely not!" as she wanted to die with all the love and respect, she had from her kids…drink was never an option. Bravely, and with great peace, after we all hugged and cried, she dozed off, and within hours, was finally at true peace. We all lost the first of our beloved siblings and friends. She asked us to take care of everyone for her…We did.

The following year, one year and week to the day of losing Joanne, we lost Jim's big brother, to a sudden heart attack. Unfortunately, our dear sister-in-law was left behind with health issues…and so our perfect world of family is slowly following life on life's terms. Jim was a rock for everyone and helped everyone. He and his sister-in-law had a special bond since Jim's drinking days and helped save his life. So, her wonderful children took care of her, and we all took our turns caring for her by either staying with her or taking her with us on trips. All so sad…

A few years later, we lost our beloved sister-in-law, and our traveling team was succumbing to life on life's terms with losses that were difficult for both our families to bear.

We knew these days were coming, but then the countdown of time hits us all. Then, there were only four of us left. We kept our promise to my sister Joanne and saw our "brother" regularly, took him to our usual vacation spots, and soon discovered he had developed serious health issues. We kept thanking God every day that Jim was doing well and helping me help everyone else…Always at the heart of our lives is our mission at the Villa…still going strong and needing us there as well as us needing it.

As we tried to keep the remainder of our siblings moving and close, we saw Jim's brother-in-law, Thomas, failing with COPD. Since he was also one of the cheerful rocks of our traveling group, and the one who always took care of Jim way back in his drinking days, this was hard to watch. His son took good care of both him and his stepmom, Ann Marie, who was doing OK at the time. Thomas became very ill and lost his battle with lung disease. It was harder and harder to keep positive as we lost another of our special group members. Tom, the eternal optimist, had always reminded us… "Don't worry…be happy!" Ann Marie and Tom's son found it hard to believe their beloved Tom… had moved on to his final happy destiny, leaving them to believe and carry on. Those of us left behind, forged ahead, bolstering each other. We honored the memories of those we lost by being there for each other and the younger folks. Jim was there for us all and was committed to being there.

Finally, one day, my brother-in-law asked me straight out, "Sue, I'm getting to my bucket list and what is on it is one more trip to Hilton Head. Can you and Jim please drive me there for a week as I love it? I promise I won't die on your watch there."

Well, the only problem was that he was getting weaker, and while his doctor said he could go as long as at the first sign of a fever, we took him to the nearest hospital, his two kids didn't think he should go. So, there we were…what could we do? Jim and I decided we were game…it was our brother, and we could do that…but what about the kids? They reluctantly said they were ok, but were worried. Long story cut short…we did it.

Driving to Hilton Head took an overnight in a motel. Also, while Jim was doing great, he could no longer drive. Thus, I was the sole driver. I didn't have any problem…I prayed hard, and it was done. At the overnight stop, we ate quickly and our brother was happy. We all decided we were going to enjoy every minute. That was his last trip. God came through and got us all there safely and home. Our Steve kept his promise not to die on my watch. He did pass away with hospice care about a month later, and we had no regrets. There was lots of sadness and more loss as he had a unique personality that kept us all on our toes. His rigidity and discipline were what got him through. It made us all admire and respect how he handled the disease he fought so courageously. Jim and I lost a brother and friend, and the kids lost their dad. We found it hard to believe Ann Marie, Jim, and myself were all that was left of that dynamic group. Our Flexible Fliers traveled all over the world together and thought it would never end… It surely went too fast.

A few more years, and we managed to get through holidays, birthdays, and events. Jim and I were grateful we had each other and were able to keep helping everyone else. Pretty soon, Ann developed severe health issues, and over the next few years, became weaker and weaker. We lost Ann in 2013, and with it, her love for life and beautiful voice. Her four sons pulled together well to keep her comfortable, and in the end, gave her a beautiful celebration of her life she had loved.

They say you don't get more than you can handle, but that one week in July 2013, tested us in every way. We lost Ann Marie, and within two days, lost two treasured members of our Villa family... Rachel and Rye. Yes, they went together and broke our hearts as well, as they left us. Here, I must share their stories with you, so you can love and treasure them as we did.

We Lost a Dear Friend and Villa Legend...Rachel

At the age of thirty, Rachel was brought over to the States by her Aunts. The year was 1950, and Rachel lived with her cousins and aunts for about four months until she found her first job in Manhasset in a large business family.

Rachel met her husband while working in the city. They married and had one daughter. Ten years later, her husband died, and she lost everything. As her addiction took over, her precious daughter was taken from her and placed in a home for adoption.

We first met Rachel in September 1978, when her friends heard the Sisters of Amityville had opened an alcohol treatment center in St. Josephs, N. Y., under the directorship of a pioneer Jim Cusack.

Rachel arrived a bit angry, but soon felt comfortable and slowly found a home with the Sisters, Jim and me. She began helping other women in treatment and soon developed our first Environmental Services department. If you were in Rachel's good graces, you would find your room quite clean and orderly. If you, for some reason, got on her wrong side, you may end up with a "short sheet" situation. She had a fabulous sense of humor and keen Irish wit just short of being brutally honest. To know her was to love her, and you could be sure of always knowing where you stood.

Years passed, and Rachel grew with us. She became an "other mother" to us as well as many clients. But she was heartbroken she had lost her daughter and finally wanted to try and find her. Jim and I hired an agency to find her, and we did. Rachel had learned earlier she had been adopted by a nice family and sent to college. By the time we found her she was married to a fine young man and had a 10-year-old boy. We called and asked if we could visit. She said ok, as long as we didn't plan any counseling. We agreed, and by the end of the evening, Rachel and her grandson, who was now age ten, the same age as Rachel's daughter was when she lost her, became fast friends. They all enjoyed many years together as Rachel saw him grow into a fine young man, and we all attended his college graduation and employment successes. He was the pride and joy of Rachel's life, and her daughter enjoyed the friendship.

Jim Cusack was one of Rachel's favorites at the Villa, and in her eyes, he could do no wrong. If she was upset with any of us, she would often say, "Let's keep it between us…don't bother Jim." She was quick to defend him and assure us all that only Jim could run the Villa and took pride in their shared Irish background. He, too, enjoyed and appreciated her honest Irish wit, so like his own.

She also took all the problem clients under her wing. She would boss them around into sobriety... all of them respecting her reprimands and not wanting to get on her wrong side.

As she retired from working at the Villa, she began to mind our dogs and home whenever we traveled... Each dog was spoiled, and they adored her for it. First, there was Totem... then Archie... then Duke. As we cried and mourned Duke when he passed, a three-year-old yellow lab, Rye, arrived for review and won all our hearts. We couldn't help but agree to have one more who desperately needed a home. He found one of Duke's toys in the yard, dropped it in Rachel's lap, and made it clear he was our dog.

He and Rachel spent many a day and night together, there at the house. Rye gave us all unconditional love for the next ten years.

Rachel and Rye were loved by all and became the center of the Villa and our lives. While Rye lived with us, he also lived for his visits by Rachel and her pockets full of biscuits. As Rachel began to fail, and for the past year was bedridden, Rye visited once in a while, and the bond was always there. Rye began to fail too, but slowly.

Rachel and Rye had a love for life, and Rachel, even though bedridden and very ill, was able to enjoy her ninety-fourth birthday with cake and all. Shortly after, she began to fail and thank everyone for all their help and kindness. She especially loved her Barbara, who was always there for her as well as nurse Gerri who she fondly called "Bubbles."

She passed saying a prayer with one of her nurses, and we were all at her bedside within minutes. We were all moved by her courage and heartbroken to have lost this special friend who touched everyone at the Villa. Her kitchen friends would prepare special treats for her every day…her maintenance friends would always be there to make sure all was OK. She showed us all how to die with dignity, courage, and grace, and we were glad to be there at the end.

We came home and explained to Rye that Rachel had passed, and he seemed to sense something had happened.

Four days later, at 5:00 a.m., we awoke to see Rye collapsing on our bedroom floor and passing within minutes. We held him and cried, and realized that Rachel and Rye were together again, and that we were blessed to have been there for him. Heartbroken as we were, it somehow all fell into place.

Rye Cusack

MAY 7, 2001 – JULY 25, 2013

Rye wasn't just a dog. He was a special family member who stole our hearts forever when he was brought to us for adoption at age three. The family, that raised him from a puppy, was forced to find a home as they had to move. They were very particular about who adopted him.

Jim and I were still grieving the loss of our beloved black lab, Duke, and weren't even sure we wanted another dog. That was quickly decided as Rachel, Jim, and I received Rye at our home. He scampered in the house, quickly found the door to the yard, ran out, and returned with one of Duke's toys that had somehow been left in the corner of the big yard. He ran in with the toy, dropped it in Rachel's lap, and it was love at first sight for us all.

His first night with us was a disaster. As we proceeded to leave the lights on for him and found out later, he was trained that all lights out meant bedtime. He was perfectly trained...not to touch anything that wasn't his when we first adopted him. That didn't last long as he claimed every wastebasket as his hunting ground for biscuits and ladies' pocketbooks and pockets as well. He was truly a food-sniffing dog but did it so lovingly he would schmooze anyone into giving him a biscuit.

The years went by, and Rye became the unconditional lover of us all. He and Rachel became fast buddies as he protected her and our house as we traveled a lot during those years. When Rachel became ill and stayed in our home with us for an entire month with oxygen, we were afraid he might eat the tubes or trip Rachel. Somehow, our Rye had an uncanny way of guiding her to her room and never once touched the tubing. He knew she needed him, and our "Prince of a Dog," as one of his veterinarians called him, rose to the role of our protector.

If any of us were sick, Rye would stay by our side...just to be there...most of the time. They were fast buddies, and if Jim were home, he would be hanging out by his side. Of course, Jim, too, was very liberal on the biscuits.

Rye developed many health issues over the years, epilepsy common to labs, and some fatty tumors. We found two great vets, one local and a surgeon in Albany. They were so kind to him, and he, of course, won them over. While not the best-behaved dog, he would do anything for a biscuit and had us all trained well.

Subsequently, we realized, as we helped Rachel through her last days with us, Rye had trouble walking, and the tumors were growing. He, still, was very active, never missed a mealtime or pill time, and eager to bring us a toy to play. His last days were also happening before our eyes, and he left us quickly, with such love and dignity that we were in shock.

At 5 a.m. on July 25, he walked into our bedroom as though it were time to go out, but he collapsed and died right there! When we called to him, he lifted his head once and left us. The only solace was that it appeared Rachel looked down from above, knew he was ready, let us have a few days to say goodbye, and then took him home with her.

Anyone who has ever loved a dog knows they are a special gift. Our hearts were broken, but we found comfort in knowing that Rachel and Rye were together again.

And so, Jim and I were last ones standing, though we were both in denial about it. We fought to find a doctor who could cure Jim's mounting ailments as Jim began a slow and insidiously cruel decline. The only gift to it was that it gave us time to prepare, to enjoy and treasure every moment as Jim was weaned away from us. It was hard to watch as he lost his sight, strength, and abilities, and we protected him avidly from losing his dignity. His love and humor were a gift to the very end... and I will share more about it later...

Jim, our brother, sister, four in-laws, and I always called ourselves the "Flexible Fliers" – always ready to go. Then, it was just me...my entire team was up there flying together. I know they would grab me up with them quickly when it was my time! Sure, do miss them all...

At this point, I want to share that our siblings left us some absolutely great nieces and nephews. They filled a void in our lives, of not being able to have our own children, and helped us both through Jim's last years with us. My sister's children and Jim's brother's children are not just nieces and nephews, but our true friends. We have been through deep joys and sorrows together and truly treasure being both family and kindred spirits. Growing up, we were like the big sister and brother to them as they were teenagers and young adults when Jim and I married. We shared in all their marriages, raising of their children, and having them trust us to take them on vacations and be the indulgent aunt and uncle. We were big kids ourselves and treasure all our memories with each and every one. I thank them, especially now, as they are always there in my memories.

All of these kids were such an important part of our lives that I had to share the fullness we experienced every time we were with them.

All of them, whoever could attend, were there for all the special birthday parties we had for Jim...

His seventy-fifth on a cruise to the Bahamas on the Queen Mary...eighteen of us for that one...

His eightieth at Canyon Ranch in the Berkshires... twenty-four there for a love-filled weekend of fun and memories...

His eighty-fifth birthday at Mohegan Sun in Connecticut... twenty-five or so of the above nieces and nephews all pulled off a surprise on this one... and Uncle Jim brought everyone luck on the machines...

Our fortieth wedding anniversary in Saratoga at the Racetrack for the weekend...full of good luck, thanks to

Uncle Jim, great food at the Wishing Well, and many other places, and full of love and fun. We were blessed to have shared so many good times.

As all these children got older, and did their own traveling, we thought surely, they would forget those moments that were such a treasure to us. How wrong we were! When we heard they were off in Disneyland, it conjured up thoughts of them doing the rides… "just one more time" … and so many more great memories. All of a sudden, out of nowhere, a text appeared on my phone of a nephew and his girlfriend on one of the many rides we took together saying … "Hi from Disneyland…thinking of you and all the fun we had." It brought tears to my eyes and we shared with everyone, the value of taking time out from work, making memories, and enjoying family.

I can't say how many times over the years all of the above kids have texted us and shared remembering the many "Birthday parties with them and our dogs"…"cereal parties late at night when they stayed over"…long trips in the car to surprise destinations…Uncle Jim promising them a nice "Bonus" if they behaved and didn't fight in the back of the car…the mornings Jim would come in early to wake them up with an ear-shattering whistle that only he could do! And the one morning they will never forget when we all got together and woke up Jim with a water spray…get even time was fun and Uncle Jim was a great sport about it. Many times, when we planned those trips, we placed business second, and some people questioned us, but we never thought twice…sometimes Jim wasn't that well, but we went anyway. Today, when we hear them all talk, we know it was worth every minute!!! Now they have the cereal parties with their own kids, make cookies, and celebrate their dogs' birthdays… we were blessed.

Our step kids are another blessing…Four great children from Jim's prior marriage… The two younger ones were very close to Jim, growing up and considered him the only dad they ever knew. When Jim and I got together, it took years of patience and prayers for them to accept us, but it was important to me because it meant so much to Jim. I could see happiness and a glow in him when we were with them. I pushed for them to be together, they pulled me in, and we shared a special love as well.

Every one of these kids have become special loves in my life, and each of the girls keep in close touch. We have the common bond of loving and treasuring one very special man…our Jim. Along with that and many weekends together celebrating Jim's birthdays, we have developed a closeness that we all value. We all actually LIKE each other and enjoy each other's company. On top of that, we can retrieve and enjoy many memories of Jim and time spent together that are a gift in itself.

While we never did experience having our own biological children, God more than made up for that love in our lives with all of the above. It was like a fast forward without all the diapers and the hard part… maybe He had it planned that way!!!

Now, you can see how great it was for us to have the love and friendship of all these great kids, as Jim and I struggled through the last years of his life. When it was time for a wedding, they would be sure Uncle Jim and I were on the first floor, as his sight was failing. If it were someone's birthday, they would be sure accommodations were made for Uncle Jim to be included…no fuss no bother…never made us feel like a burden. When he needed a walker or wheelchair, everyone made light of it… just glad to have us there for him to continue to love them and spoil them. Everyone was graced by Uncle Jim's generosity as he always had a few extra dollars for each one and would "slip them something" … "just between them." With the dollar was Uncle Jim's unending pride of them all and them wanting to be like him or measure up to his expectations. As he aged and his sight and awareness failed, someone often received $100 bills instead of 50s or 20s and everyone adhered to the honor system and let Aunt Sue know. We, and me in particular, were blessed, to enjoy the love and care of them all as Jim's time neared an end.

Jim's last birthday, April 26, 2016, we celebrated at home with an all-day open house for all family, staff, and friends to visit…he was as happy as possible. Hospice was in the background, but since Jim was in no pain…just weakness from heart and organ failure, we had his favorite sugar free cake from Deisings, lots of delicious catered food, lots of attention and hugs, and he ate well and enjoyed it all. It was a big joke, and he had his sense of humor and Irish charm intact. He would pull aside his nephew or one of our staff and say, "Hey, Sue's not looking, grab me an extra Reese's peanut butter…she's worried about my sugar, but it's really OK."

By the end of the day, he thoroughly had enjoyed about twenty Reese's, along with extra cake, and I pretended to see nothing and just be happy that he was happy. By this time, the doctors had given up on me, too, watching every bit of salt and sugar he ate. His happiness for the day was more important.

A few days later, he had a bad fall on his hip as he was trying to surprise me and walk out to the kitchen himself instead of waiting for me to help. He was always worried about my health…always telling me how much he loved me and was sorry to be the way he was. Heartbroken, I assured him I was glad to have him there with me, anyway he was, and that every minute together was a treasure. I had vowed never to leave him in the hospital as he felt safe with me, and his lack of eyesight wasn't noticed by the average person. Our love, which started with such a spark of intensity, was then deep burning embers, still so much alive with the spark, deeper than ever. When days began to fill with fear, waking us both in the middle of the night, we held hands, just to be sure we were still there for each other. During the day, when we would be overwhelmed with the unknown, we often just hugged and cried, and assured each other how grateful we were for the day. Somehow, with all our prayers and rosaries, I managed to be there and did not get sick myself. That had become my biggest fear. God was good and kept me well.

The fall on the hip that day was bad, as it indicated he was losing more and more muscle control. I had to call someone to help me get Jim to the chair. We had to call an ambulance to be sure nothing was broken. My biggest fear was taking him to the hospital as we had hospice in place, and extra help as well, for his comfort and peace of always being at home with me. When the fall left the question of a broken hip, we had no recourse but to check it out.

Our niece, who is the director of another hospital, met us there. After the ER doctors assured us there was no break, they hit me with what I already knew... Jim was in the final stages of dying, his organs were failing, and it was just a matter of time. To actually hear it was heartbreaking, but then came the next phase of our final journey together. The doctors called our niece aside, suggested I leave Jim in hospital, and asked her, "Does his wife know he is dying?" We both said yes and that I have hospice in place and want to make his last days comfortable and with me. The ER doctor was very supportive as he had just made a similar decision for his own dad and mom and admired our courage. It was a relief to know someone in the medical field understand that when they can no longer fix someone, leave them to be loved.

So, I signed Jim out of the hospital, hired our own ambulance, and brought him home to our own bed, and helped me get him tucked in for the night. We shared an ice cream in bed that night and slept as best we could, facing the final unknown in our lives together. God knows there were many unknowns from the first day we stepped off the plane in Haiti to our wedding!

Now for the final tear-filled chapter...

Our staff at the Villa were wonderful, compassionate, and there for us both. People visited, shared a stolen candy, chatted, and assured Jim he was needed and loved. My friends at our local hospital found me a male nurse to help me get Jim to bed at night. The rest of the time, we could maneuver ourselves with walkers and chairs, laughing many times at our clumsiness and Jim stealing a kiss when he could! His charm and beautiful blue eyes remained as did his passion for helping others.

Another week went by, and he became more uncomfortable, but still no pain. Walking became a major issue, and we kept up with our visitors and special food they would bring. His last weekend, we began with our usual Friday night Chinese food dinner brought in by our faithful friends Rick (sober since Jim's first place in 1965) and his friend, Geraldine, who ate with us and cheered us and overlooked Jim's frailty. His appetite was great that night, and he ate all the salty food that would no longer make a difference. The next day was a nightmare as Jim couldn't get comfortable, and even though we opted for hospice, we were never prepared when to administer the final comfort medications that would ease his passing. Just one more day… I wished…his heart doctor kept saying, "Get him up to feed him."

Hospice said, "Be ready to leave him in bed, comfortable," all the while praying and sprinkling holy water, wishing for a miracle. He slept like a baby all day, woke up at midnight saying "Sue, I feel great! let's pack up the car and go on a little trip…I feel so good." It was like he felt this thing chasing him and me, and he wanted us to escape! Oh, how I wished I could…like we were both always good at taking off and taking risks together…escaping a bad week, getting away from bad weather, but we couldn't escape death that was really at our heels. While my heart wanted to grab him and run, I said, "Let's celebrate your feeling so good with a big Kit Kat bar in bed, and let me get some rest first and we'll leave in the morning." He couldn't believe I actually gave him a big candy bar like that and enjoyed every bit. He slept well that night, and the next day was the day I was never prepared for. Then, I knew he was on his way without me, and I prayed for the strength to let go. It was the rainiest Sunday ever…my niece and nephew, who always came over on Saturday, couldn't make it that Saturday, and were with me on that Sunday. They were also good friends who made sure they saw us EVERY Saturday for a movie or dinner, however Jim was capable of going…walker or wheelchair…faithfully, for the last two years.

God's hand was already at work. Providentially, they were there for me and able to give me quiet support as we all knew the time was near. All I wanted to do was be near him. Around 4:00 p.m., I felt a peace and calm come over me, and I remembered where I had tucked away a brown scapular, my friend Mary had given me. I hated her for it at the time, as I felt it was a bad omen even though we all knew Jim was dying. When she gave it to me, she said that "anyone wearing this at the time they die, are assured of being swooped up directly into heaven… no doubt about it." I kept it out of sight for the longest time. Then, as I searched for it and found it, I also found I was releasing Jim to God, and it broke my heart. I held the scapular in my hand, cried my eyes out, walked over to my sleeping Jim…oh so comfortable and peaceful…and gently placed it over his head and around his neck. I kissed him and prayed to God and his mom and dad to take care of him, as they asked me to, a long time ago. I prayed, "God, please let it be peaceful and beautiful for him." Our beloved priest friend Fr. Sal came over in the rainstorm to give Jim a final blessing. He hugged us all, prayed and left. I went in to see the kids for a bit, assured them I was OK and went back to sit by the bed and just BE near Jim and hold his hand. I felt at peace and full of love, but oh so tearful. My niece came in behind me and stood a bit. Just at that moment, Jim raised his head, turned towards me, opened his big beautiful blue eyes for the last time, opened his mouth as though trying to say goodbye, and that was my last gift from the best gift in my life.

He was able to hold my hand and say goodbye. I will never forget that day, nor will my niece, who was a witness to it all. She had lost her daughter to the tragedy of an epileptic seizure, and it renewed her faith in the spirit world. We all cried our eyes out as we held him for the last time, Kenneth was also there, and we said our goodbyes.

It was all final, and now there was a lot to do. I felt overwhelmed and requested my two nephews to take over and help me make decisions about arrangements. I wanted everything to be special for Jim, but the reality of why it had to be so, was devastating. A part of me…THE WE…had died forever. He was eighty-seven years old…we were married forty-four beautiful years…we were given much more than I had ever hoped for, but it was never enough time. I knew the only way to continue was to find gratitude in this entire heartache…

All the family, kids, friends, and staff were fantastic…couldn't do enough and were all grieving in their own way. Even all our step kids came from near and far…nieces and nephews traveled and stayed to be there for Uncle Jim and now, Aunt Sue. It is said that what goes around comes around, and I was, and am grateful that all the love Jim gave to all came back to him and us that day.

We all agreed that Jim had lost a lot of weight, and we should probably have a closed casket, with his handsome smiling picture nearby. But Jim had one more surprise and gift of love to let me know he was still here with me. He always loved to dress smartly for work with suit and tie. Even though I thought no one would see, I selected his beautiful yellow shirt, Hermes tie, and dark suit.

The funeral home directors, a lovely caring couple, suggested that before we close the casket, I make that final decision when I saw him. When I went in with my nieces and nephews at my side, I WAS AMAZED AT HOW HANDSOME AND GLOWING HE LOOKED! We all cried tears of joy as he gave me the last gift of being physically present…right there with me…for his last goodbyes! No one could get over how handsome and peaceful our Jim looked. His final gift then but now I know he would send many more surprises from the spirit world…just to let me know he kept his promise to never leave me. What comfort those times were…a song that was special…many little things that assure me he was just waiting for me so we could "get away together" and pick up where we had left.

Jim's wake was a beautiful tribute of people, love for him, and the life he lived…hundreds coming to say thank you. By the grace of God, I was able to stand by him as he lay there…to thank each and every one who came and cried with them. His funeral began with the military send-off he would have been proud of, followed by a Mass and a eulogy by his beloved friend, Fr. Steven, and our nephew, who Jim once held in his arms as a baby. It was a blur of the deepest sadness I have ever known, with a gathering afterward and home to the emptiness that was now to be my life. My faith got me through the next few days, along with dear family and friends, but the hole in my heart was raw, and I couldn't stop crying. A week later, my dear brother and friend, Lee, from the Villa suggested I just come over to the Villa on a Sunday…ease my way back to what was Jim's and my life and creation… The Villa. Our dedicated and committed staff had kept the Villa going during the time I was home, taking care of Jim for the last six months or so. I am forever grateful for that precious time with him.

Soon after the funeral, I realized the stark reality of the promise, Jim and I once made to each other… whomever of us was left behind would carry on the Villa. But I was lost without him…how can this be…where do I begin? Somehow, I had always thought God would realize how much we were soul mates and needed not to be separated by death. Somehow, I thought we would die in a plane crash together…or in many of the daring things we would try…like helicopters through the Grand Canyon… car rides during a blizzard over the fiords in Iceland…but no…there was my Jim… on the other side, and finally in perfect peace and love that I wanted for him… and there I was…left behind…to face another chapter in my life…the page was empty and scary.

One Sunday, I ventured my way over to the Villa and began talking to the families, as Jim and I always did. Something kicked into my inner soul, and I could feel Jim and I together in spirit reaching out to whomever I was talking to. It was Jim's spirit, pushing me beyond myself doing the work and mission we both loved. By "bringing the body" as we tell people in our Twelve Steps meetings "the mind will follow." And it began again for me…a renewal and love for the mission…our child…the Villa…and myself…were to continue. While I cried every Sunday, when I spoke to the families, they accepted (many had known Jim and understood), and cried with me. Each Sunday got a little easier, and before long, while still heartbroken, I felt I was doing what Jim would want me to do…and that the veil between him and me was thinner, and I often found myself quoting him.

A few months had gone by, and the cruel world of widowhood crept in…many harsh reminders that Jim was really gone…Social Security forces you to meet with them to change status…a doctor's office asks you…marital status and you have to say the tragic words…"widow"…That couldn't be me, but yes, it was…Many mechanical things of everyday life must be recorded and changed, and I found myself not wanting to but had to.

Then there was all his clothing and belongings…they hung in the closet…the shirts he loved to wear…precious jewelry…I wore his wedding ring since the night he died and still do, behind my engagement ring he was proud he could finally surprise me with after sixteen years married!

For a long time, there was a comfort in going into the closet and feel the shirts near me…then after a while, seeing them was a raw reminder…He was never coming back to wear them. Then the thought entered, *"What would Jim want me to do?"* And I began passing on his favorite colored sweaters, our nephews always admired and loved, to the nephews and nieces who treasured them as much as I did. The first Christmas without Jim was the tremendous loss I knew it would be. Christmas was always our favorite holiday, and we would love to surprise each other. Then, I knew the family needed me to be there, and the Villa needed me to carry on the love and joy, Jim and I always looked forward to sharing.

Christmas found me tearfully passing on some treasured jewelry belonging to Jim that would soon be a meaningful treasure to someone who loved him. It gave me peace to know, rather than sitting in a drawer, both Jim and I would be passing on a part of him in love and joy.

I found myself leaning on the philosophy of our beautiful Twelve Steps program given to me by Jim in the early days of my recovery. One day at a time…sometimes one minute at a time…passing into months of my new life alone. I applied the Steps…Step 1 being powerless over widowhood and my life was unmanageable …over time as I admitted this, I could learn to accept it…but Step 2… came to believe a power greater than myself could restore me to sanity…gave me hope that I wouldn't always feel this lost and alone…slowly, I could find joy in small things and be grateful for all I enjoyed with Jim, Step 3…made a decision to turn my will and life over to the care of God, as I understood Him…every morning I got into a discipline and routine of beginning the day with my two J.C.'s…Jesus Christ and Jim Cusack. Sister Mary gave me a book soon after Jim died entitled "Jesus Calling" … which I thought was similar to God calling, but one day, I picked it up and began to make Jesus my new best friend along with Jim. Most times, the messages for the day were uncanny and helped me focus my day in peace and alignment with my spirit world. Step 4…made a searching and fearless moral inventory…helped me take inventory of all the years I've enjoyed… forty-four with Jim when I first had hoped for at least twenty-five! What a gift it all was…so much I could lean on and take into the years ahead…however many I may have. Step 5…admitted to God, ourselves and another human being the exact nature of our wrongs…as time went on, I kept going like a robot…worked very hard and kept busy so I wouldn't have to think and grieve. Luckily friends, Sister Peg, and Sister Mary noticed, and gently gave me a retreat gift for those who have loved and lost…A Beginning Experience Retreat. I accepted graciously, wondering how it could help. It truly was what I needed, and by doing the fifth step, I found a new freedom and peace with Jim closer in a new way. The sixth and seventh steps helped me to share more openly with my friends and staff, and ask them openly for feedback on seeing myself as others see me. Not easy to do, but I was amazed as I learned more and more how to be a better me.

Jim had always taught us to do this and made himself very vulnerable and open, which many admired. Suddenly I found the strength in this and new peace within myself. Not perfect at it but aware and a work in progress. Step 8…made a list of all persons we had harmed and became willing to make amends to them all. Doing this in my daily life forced me to reach out to others and see where I failed them as I was grieving and lost touch with people along the way. It was taking time, and again, it was a work in progress. Step 9…made direct amends to such people, wherever possible, except to do so would injure them or others. Again, as time moved on and I became more aware of those around me, the list became shorter. Step 10…my favorite at the end of the day…continued to take personal inventory, and when I was wrong, promptly admitted it. Being comfortable with myself is my best thermometer for checking on me at the end of the day. If I have an uncomfortable feeling as to how I handled someone or a situation, I call them immediately…even if it's late at night…another character defect I am working on.

Step 11…Sought through prayer and meditation to improve my conscious contact with God as I understand Him, praying only for knowledge of His will and the power to carry that out. This perhaps is the most important step for me today, as I feel more and more the responsibility for carrying on the Villa…taking care of the staff, giving them what they need to work and grow comfortably, taking care of clients, and giving them the compassion and direction they need, making sure we remain true to the core philosophy Jim set in place, maintaining the Villa physical plant, adhering to regulations except when to do so would injure them or others according to our philosophy…innumerable things to consider. Since I believe God works and directs me through other people, I do lean on outside advisors who I respect and admire, along with trusted staff who have the Villa close to their heart. Step 12…Having had a spiritual awakening as a result of viewing these precious steps once again, I carry this message to the addicted and PRACTICE THESE PRINCIPLES IN ALL MY/ OUR AFFAIRS.

What a great way of life…what a set of guidelines to live up to…as long as I live, I find all the answers to my troubles, sadness, even my greatest loss of living without Jim. These steps have always given me the steel I need to go on…and I know they will continue as long as I make the effort to practice them always.

During all of the above, with a broken heart, I was committed to keeping the Villa going no matter what. As I backed into managing it once again, bringing back the hopes and dreams Jim and I had planned for its future, I had to refer often to the title of Jim's book… "Trouble is a gift."

The roof over the women's dining room collapsed, and rain poured in during our first hurricane of the season…customers missed Jim's generous policy of telling all "just come on up"…insurance began to dictate treatment…the brokering of clients began sending people to Florida rather than Kerhonkson…our census was dwindling to below ten by Christmas the first year without Jim. Staff support held firm and I with them. While money was tight, we never missed a payroll, and my promise to Jim was to get its first big test. Somehow, with many prayers and lots of holy water, we managed to make it through. I personally called all our business friends and associates and asked if they could help the Villa name get back on track. At all our staff meetings that first year, we focused on compassionate customer and client care. Slowly they visited, we heard their complaints and needs, and we got their promises and commitment to help us.

During the first snowstorm of the season, we saw our plow break down as it became a whiteout snowfall…we scrambled as we had to hire neighbors to get us through. We doctored our old plow through and were blessed with very little snow for the rest of the season. Year two found us shopping for a decent truck and snowplow as our new team learned how to keep prepared.

The first year we lost three more key and treasured residents and rock stars of the Villa. The first was our driver, 5-year resident, and dear friend to Jim and me. Harry B. was found dead in his room of a sudden heart attack. He was one of a kind and missed very much. Months later, we lost our dear friend, Jean Barbara M., another special resident who touched many lives. She helped Jim with his book, kept scores of alumni close to her always, touched us all with her good nature, sense of humor and love of family and friends. She always made sure all the holidays were special and decorated and took care of many things we still miss.

A few months later, we lost Andrew F…a longtime friend to all. He, too, like Jean, always had the Villa's mission front and foremost… Andrew always stepped in for phones, snack time for clients, talking to everyone, and our best unofficial counselor. Like Jean, everyone knew and trusted Andrew and knew he was always available for a call, a pat on the back, or a kick-in-the-you-know-what as needed.

Losing Harry, Jean, and Andrew, soon after Jim, left us in shock, as they were always there to pick us up and assure us Jim would be proud… "we are doing well" … "give ourselves a pat on the back that all would be OK." It was like losing your favorite aunts and uncles who were always there for you and made sure all was OK. The new staff is picking up the care, but we still miss them all very much.

The second year, we attempted to paint the entire Villa…that went from $65,000 estimate with no real lasting repairs to a final $325,000 total siding and beautiful finish thanks to our Bank loan. But the compliments and obvious statement to all that we are here for the long haul are well worth it.

Thanks to getting youth involved in our staff, we worked closely with a local radio station and national website company, and revamped our entire website last year, which vamped us up on Google and gave us a working web that reaches new people every day. Now, all across country, people are googling and finding their way to Kerhonkson when fitting. We have also learned how to maximize our Villa Facebook to keep up with all our alumni and their friends. It's truly a new world out there!

Our peers, businesses, and union friends have been an invaluable source of strength and support and continually help us keep on top of things. We stick together as we all try to keep compassion, ethics, and basic values in our treasured field.

Above all couldn't have managed without the emotional love and support of our families...the calls, texts, emails, visits, and constant daily contact means more than I could ever say.

Jim's memory lives on in all of us and several in the field. Jim is always referred to as a pioneer, one of a kind who lived to serve and help the addict and their family.

When you walk into the Villa now, three years since his passing, you will feel his spirit if you knew him, and if you didn't know him, our CARF accrediting organization said she felt a SPIRIT here that she walked through twice to experience...a SPIRIT she said was unique...one we should "get out there" and advertise. This from an accrediting body of people who go all over the country...she felt the spirit we know is our Jim.

Truly Love is stronger than death…and Jim is still here…believing that has helped us through these first three years without him.

Over these past years, we have developed a phenomenal staff fully capable of running the Villa without me, though I have no intention of retiring…ever! As long as I am healthy and able doing what I love with the people I love keeps me going…as it did Jim. We were blessed to be able to make a difference in someone's life.

Thanks to Mom's Holy Water in My Scotch, I celebrated fifty years sober on June 5, 2019! It was bittersweet yet meaningful as it was the third anniversary of Jim's passing. I knew he would want me to celebrate to share that it can be done. I knew he was proud that I did.

We celebrated in my home Group in High Falls, NY, and my first sponsor, who drove me to the hospital on June 5, 1969, gave me Jim's fiftieth-year coin. She is ninety-five and a blessing to all. My sister-in-law and her husband surprised me, along with many dear friends.

I'm sure Mom was smiling …as the Holy Water keeps working. And the Mission continues ….

AS FOR THE FUTURE OF THE VILLA… What are our dreams and vision for the Villa of tomorrow?

As we look back and see how we have been led and the Villa has evolved, we first take our requests to the Auriesville Shrine, where we have always gone. Then we come back and pray we are open to the ideas and people yet to be led our way.

After surviving the past three years without Jim and the many drastic changes in our field, we are finally at a time we can begin to look ahead.

We would like to reach all the people who don't know we are here…families who don't realize they have a disease…if we could help more people, we will be able to add staff benefits and have the best cared for staff in the field.

We would like to utilize more of our unused 100 acres of property to help more families, maybe family retreat centers, and a separate new building for women! One day those doors will open… Jim talked a lot about utilizing our property before he passed away, but it was and still is an urging. Perhaps now he can direct us from above. Maybe someone will appear soon to show us the way.

Overall our dream is still the eleventh step, seek through prayer and meditation, knowledge of His will for us and the power to carry it out; continue to put people first, dollars second, treat all with compassion and kindness as we teach the values and discipline that helped us stay sober.

Our wildest dreams include a new building on the mountain, a separate women's building, focus on what our true mission is, and never to grow too large to keep the personal touch.

We pray our visionary, Jim, continues to lead us from above, and keep us humble, as we keep true to the ethics and principles crucial to our spiritual health as a treatment center and nation.

We thank Jim and all who taught him…especially his sponsor Joe L. and his mom and pop Cusack.

I am honored God chose me to be Jim's soulmate and partner in this mission and journey beyond our wildest dreams…we sure enjoyed our trip together and I will continue, as long as my two J.C.'s have planned.

AS FOR MY PERSONAL FUTURE… I pray God gives me the health and wisdom to help all who come through our doors on a personal basis to find help and hope. I need them more than they need me because each one is a gift which gives me new energy. Being in the trenches with our family program every week helps me connect through my past pain and offer them hope…seeing them leave with a smile and some hope for their loved one revitalizes us every week. Addressing families on Sundays is another gift, especially seeing their children discover Mom or Dad are truly good people with a bad disease. When a nine-year old can stand and announce that he could separate his mom from the disease and love her…there is no better gift.

I also pray to continue to be a big part of all my treasured nieces, nephews, and step-children's lives, be their cheerleader and biggest fans, watch them marry, have children, and continue to be able to play hide and seek and several games with them. I hope I can be half the friend to all the couple friends and single friends who have been there for me since I lost Jim. I thank them all for including me, keeping me going, and loving me. They have all taught me I can laugh and have fun again as Jim would want me to.

We hope this book will offer hope, help, and give purpose to all who read. When I wrote a prayer of petition to God at the Auriesville Shrine, in 1971, I had no idea how he would answer and how he would use my joys and sorrows to help many. My life has been truly a gift beyond my plans and helps me to wonder what other great things He has around the corner! I pray with positive expectation every day, am often amazed at what happens and when and

I know one day, Jim is… "just around the corner…waiting for me."